The Henry L. Stimson Lectures Series

THE IMPRINT OF CONGRESS

DAVID R. MAYHEW

Yale
UNIVERSITY PRESS
New Haven and London

The Henry L. Stimson Lectures at the Whitney and Betty MacMillan Center for International and Area Studies at Yale.

Published with assistance from the foundation established in memory of James Wesley Cooper of the Class of 1865, Yale College.

Yale University Press books may be purchased in quantity for educational, business, or promotional use. For information, please e-mail sales. press@yale.edu (U.S. office) or sales@yaleup.co.uk (U.K. office).

Set in Adobe Garamond and Gotham type by IDS Infotech Ltd. Printed in the United States of America.

ISBN 978-0-300-21570-0 (hardcover : alk. paper)

Library of Congress Control Number: 2016955268

A catalogue record for this book is available from the British Library.

This paper meets the requirements of ANSI/NISO Z39.48–1992 (Permanence of Paper).

10 9 8 7 6 5 4 3 2 1

Contents

To my wife Judith
and our dog
Tiger

Acknowledgments

This book started as a conference paper and grew. Many thanks to Gregory Wawro and Ira Katznelson for posing a question to paper writers for a conference on "Congress and History" held at Columbia University on June 21–22, 2013. That charge jogged me to action. The question was: "Can Congress as a 'core institution' of American democracy capably address the major challenges confronting the nation at any given period?" A shorter version was "Can Congress govern?" I took the phrase "at any given period" to invite a canvass of history. A paper ensued. It grew longer in a version published in *Studies in American Political Development* in October 2015, where the title was "Congress as a Handler of Challenges: The Historical Record." This book is a reconfiguration and expansion of the project. Thanks to the Stimson Lectures at Yale University, and to Yale University Press, for allowing it. Matching the reconfiguration, there is a fresh title, *The Imprint of Congress*. The discursive freedom that a book affords, compared with a conference paper or a journal article, is a considerable joy. Along the way, I have profited from advice from Richard Bensel, Sarah Binder, David Brady, Jacob Hacker, David Karol, Ira Katznelson, Joseph LaPalombara, Nuno Monteiro, William Nordhaus, Eleanor Powell, Eric Schickler, Ian Shapiro, Stephen Skowronek, Judith Swanson, Richard Valelly, Steven Wilkinson, and anonymous referees. Thanks to Charles Kromkowski for data he sent me a few years ago in an earlier cause. A visit to Jack Balkin's class at the Yale Law School was bracing and rewarding. As always, thanks to the Yale University Library system. My research assistants, Matt Bettinger and John A. Dearborn, did valiant service in checking the manuscript at various phases for its sources and mistakes and in designing displays. Dearborn arranged the nine figures that appear in this work.

Introduction

What has been Congress's imprint on American society and life? I wrestle with this question in this book. It is a tough question, but, I believe, an interesting one. To address it, I lay out some rules of analysis and invite the reader to go along with them.

It is a distinctive question. There are alternative questions. Many are chestnuts of public affairs that I am *not* asking here: Has Congress been democratic or representative enough?[1] Have its processes been suitably fair, efficient, or all-around edifying? Has Congress been good at passing White House proposals? Have Americans liked the way Congress performs? *No!* is a pretty clear answer to the last of these questions: Across eighty-some years of public opinion surveys, the ratings show a low average, a good deal of volatility, and no long-term slope up or down that you would want to take to the bank (although recent years have brought some especially low figures).[2] Americans have not been fans of congressional performance.

American intellectuals—journalists, academics, and the rest—have not been fans, either. There is a long tradition of critique.[3] Many difficulties have been aired. In 1885, Woodrow Wilson, pioneering the genre in his classic *Congressional Government,* saw the House of Representatives as obstructionist, opaque, particularistic, unaccountable, given to meddling in executive administration, poor at debate, prone to poor policies, and "servile" to "the whims of popular constituencies."[4] The

House, the British scholar James Bryce wrote in his influential 1888 account, "tends to avoid all really grave and pressing questions."[5] The Senate of the mid-twentieth century hosted, to cite another kind of problem, "the ravages of McCarthyism," in the words of Walter Lippmann.[6]

A lineage of book titles tells the story: *Congress at the Crossroads* (1946), *Congress on Trial* (1949), *The Deadlock of Democracy* (very much about Congress, 1963), *Obstacle Course on Capitol Hill* (1964), *The Sapless Branch* (1964), *Congress in Crisis* (an analysis of the critique tradition rather than a critique itself, 1966), *The American Way of Politics at the Breaking Point* (very much about Congress, 1996), *Fight Club Politics* (2006), *The Broken Branch* (2006).[7] Congress's inertia, perhaps the most familiar of criticisms, can be seen in a long line of terminology. James MacGregor Burns set the tone in a 1949 work: "stalled," "stymied," "stalemate," "inaction," "inertness," "obstructionism," "stasis," "roadblock," "deadlock."[8] Without bothering to chase other references we might add "drift," "bottleneck," "logjam," and the now ubiquitous "gridlock." Declinism, a view that the old days were better, is a theme in many accounts. Wilson was already using the notion in the 1880s.[9] A lost golden age is sometimes spied in the courtly Senate of the 1950s, the realm of Georgia's Richard Russell and others.[10] Recently, the "distortion," "eschewal," "abandonment," "decline," "demise," and "collapse" of venerable Capitol Hill procedures were sighted in a critique by Thomas E. Mann and Norman J. Ornstein in 2006.[11] These days, the term *dysfunction* is serving as an umbrella negative trope.[12]

In this book, I sidestep this literature of critique. If you are expecting another work like that, stop right here. I sidestep it for three reasons. First, this literature tends to be driven by the aches, anxieties, and headlines of the day. Connections to a more general historical experience tend to be lean. Second, it is a literature that explains things—its insights have often been excellent—yet also, in an ideological or partisan sense, at least by strong implication, it grouses or advocates. It tends toward a blend of the positive and the normative. All very well. But we need to be on our toes. It is good to be aware, for example, that Woodrow Wilson was a Democrat of southern background, that he correspondingly saw the centralizing, Republican-run federal government of the post–Civil War years as over-the-top hyperactive in policy terms and that he proceeded to hammer Congress in his 1885 scholarship at least partly for that reason. Blame that era's disagreeable Republican policies—high tariffs, big spending, infrastructure investment, civil rights guarantees in the South, and the rest—on the government's, and especially Congress's, structure and processes. In good part, that was Wilson's animation and his analytic package.[13]

Wilson set a style. In our own times, since the 1930s, a chronic backstory to the congressional critiques is that the policy aims of liberals or Democrats often falter on Capitol Hill. There must be a reason. Culprit processes are found. It is a short step to the view: "My party can't get what it wants, so the system must be broken." A liberal president facing a conservative Congress has become a sure bet, even if not the only bet, for system-is-broken stories. In general, a blend of the positive and the normative can pose analytic confusion. From Woodrow Wilson onward, the critique literature is best seen as a cross between, on the one hand, professional social science, and, on the other hand, a nonstop participation in national ideological warfare.

But my third reason is the chief one. I want to examine a different terrain. The critique literature tends to dwell on aspirations, processes, and optics: On the latter front, "ugliness" and "spectacle" are some of its recent terms.[14] I want to look beyond these frames into the *effects* or *results* of congressional activities—at least some of them. It is a consequentialist enterprise. Steer past the policy aspirations and drives, the internal processes, the wrangling, the repellent sausage-making or non-making as legislative ideas are considered, and where are we? Beyond that, steer past the churn of roll calls and the notching of victories and losses. Processes, so what? What are the *effects* of passing or not passing laws, of Congress's operations in general?

I construe this quest for effects as an investigation into deep history. I go back to the very beginning of the country in 1789. I sift Congress's effects on American society from those of the presidency, insofar as that is possible, and I cradle the analysis in the experience of peer countries. Through these moves, I look for distinctive congressional effects across two and a quarter centuries. This makes for a loose speculative analysis. It requires many personal judgments. There is nothing statistical about it. Also, the analysis cannot say much about the present day. I stay away from policy excitements that have flashed into prominence very recently and thus do not have much of an analyzable arc of life. As for the future, all inferences from history are of course uncertain. Doomsters are sometimes right, and who knows? Today's congressional doomsters may be right too. But in framing the past I aim for a perspective that is worth consulting at the present time.

What has been Congress's distinctive imprint? I use the term *imprint* advisedly. I mean to connote effects that are longer-lasting and more deeply embedded than would be signaled by, say, the term *impact*. I mean a congressional imprint on such states of affairs as the launching of the country in the 1790s, the coming of the regulatory state, the rise of the United States to world power, the building of the welfare state, the post–World War II civil rights revolution, the onset of economic neoliberalism around 1980, and, in the past few decades,

4

the management of federal debt and deficits. Perhaps we all have curbstone takes on big topics like these, but I believe that they are worth addressing square-on. Also, I believe that they can be addressed reasonably well at this time. This book could not have been written thirty years ago—or, if written, it would have relied on that time's conventional wisdoms about history, many of which have since flagged, and it would have been much scantier. Recent decades have brought a wonderful efflorescence of historical scholarship that I am able to call on for this project. The economic history alone is priceless.

It is not that multitudes of scholars have addressed Congress as their main topic, although certainly some have. It is that many have hit on Congress somehow, offering an insight along the way, as they have pursued their own main topics. I have taken great pleasure in ferreting out such insights from a wide variety of literature—much of it, though of course not all of it, recent. What can be said today about the United States reentering the British trading area in the 1790s, or the coming of progressive taxation, or the righting of the economy in the 1930s? Where was Congress? I have written this book, let it be said, entirely out of secondary sources. No apologies. To be serious students of Congress, we need to know what has been going on in the wide, rich secondary scholarship that touches on congressional history.

Two general concerns of political science inform this study. Both locate the United States in comparative perspective. The first is regime stability and legitimacy. Presidential systems, with their unending friction between independent executive and legislative branches, taken in contrast with parliamentary systems, are often thought to be especially unstable.[15] Who would ever have designed a system in that contradictory, conflict-inviting way? Yet the American separation-of-powers system—granted, there was the Civil War—has been *extraordinarily* stable. It is not even close. The American system is often seen, along with the British, as the gold standard for long-running constitutional stability.

Although silences are hard to interpret, this record seems to signal popular legitimacy. I mean, with a nod to Locke and Weber, legitimacy in the overarching, not easily measurable sense of being popularly bought-into as suitable and authoritative. In these terms, the American regime seems as rock-solid as, say, Switzerland's or Sweden's. Grumping about the government is an American pastime. Conflict runs on endlessly about policies, government performance, an insolent "establishment," and second-order processes like campaign finance and legislative districting. Reforms of such processes, and the drives to achieve them, are a trademark of the regime.[16] Yet where, outside the occasional academic common-room discussion, have you heard much in the way of let's-scrap-it-all questioning of the country's basic constitutional institutions—or, for that matter, the country's geographic composition? On the latter point, compare the threatened ungluing of today's Britain, Spain, or Canada.[17] We experience these basic U.S. institutions—the presidency, Congress, and the courts—and this U.S. geography as fish experience the water. Overwhelmingly, American seize on winning elections, not on overhauling the Constitution, as a tonic for whatever difficulties come along.[18]

I will argue that Congress through its operations across history has probably helped legitimize—and keep legitimized—the U.S. regime out there among the public. We don't readily see that effect, but it is likely there.

As for the legitimacy of Congress taken by itself, abstracted from the Constitution's three-ring institutional ensemble, that question is hard to address. Perhaps it cannot be addressed well. On the one hand, the public routinely pans Congress's job performance, its policy decisions or non-decisions, and its practices like pork-barreling, filibustering, and grubbing for campaign money. There is no question about it. Thumbs down is the reflexive call.

On the other hand, there can be a shrewd public appreciation of Congress. Consider the national survey data in table 1. The table draws on questions that have been asked to the public (only spottily, alas, so far as I can tell) across the last six decades, specifically during the presidencies of Dwight Eisenhower, Jimmy Carter, and George W. Bush. In principle, the three questions in the top section of the table ask, in a family of word formulations that try to guard the answers from pollution by not mentioning particular politicians or parties: Who should be making policies, Congress or the president? It is a basic question. The answer is overwhelmingly Congress, in 1958, 1977, and 2004–05. There is no time trend to the answers. Article One of the Constitution, the assignment of legislative power to Congress, seems to stay firmly embedded in the popular mind. In the face of Congress's rarely impressive job ratings, not to mention the country's long, several-generation march toward White House assertion, why might that be? The bottom section of table 1 offers some clues. The two questions shown there, plus one of those above, draw from an especially elaborate study of public opinion conducted by the Annenberg Public Policy Center in 2004–05. In the back of it all, it appears, the public sees constitutional checks and balances as a good thing and congressional conflict as, well, a natural outcome of political life. Those results seem to cut to the core. At the least, they are suggestive.

The second concern of political science that I key on is comparative, cross-country performance. I aim to compare and assess Congress's imprint as well as to discern it. I go about that in a complicated, roundabout way. Compared with peer national systems elsewhere

Table 1. How the Public Sees Congress's Role

Who should make policies, Congress or the President?

1958 – Asked during a Republican Presidency (Eisenhower), Democratic Congress: "Some people say the President is in the best position to see what the country needs. Other people think the President may have good ideas about what the country needs, but it is up to the Congress to decide what ought to be done. How do you feel about this?" (NES)

17% – President | 61% – Congress | 22% – Equal, Don't know, No answer

1977 – Asked during a Democratic Presidency (Carter), Democratic Congress: "In general, who do you think should have the most say in the way our government is run, the Congress or the President?" (CBS/NYT)

26% – President | 58% – Congress | 16% – About equal, Not sure, No answer

2004–5 – Asked during a Republican Presidency (Bush 43), Republican Congress: "When it comes to making important policy decisions, do you think that decisions should be made by the Congress or by the President?" (Annenberg)

21% – President | 59% – Congress | 14% – Both, Other

What about Congress's processes?

2004–5 – Two questions asked during a Republican presidency (Bush 43), Republican Congress:

"Which view is closer to yours—legislative checks are good, or legislative checks cause gridlock and inaction?" (Annenberg)

70% – Checks are good | 20% – Cause gridlock and inaction | 10% – Other

"Which one do you agree with most? A) Conflict is a natural part of the legislative process, or B) Members create conflict where there need not be any." (Annenberg)

63% – Conflict a natural part | 32% – Need not be any | 5% – Other

Sources: National Election Study (NES) 1958, question V580154; CBS/New York Times Poll, April 1977; Princeton Survey Research Associates International (PSRAI) national survey conducted in December 2004 and January 2005 as part of the Institutions of American Democracy Project, Annenberg Public Policy Center, University of Pennsylvania, respectively questions 3, 30, and 34c.

across history, how has the U.S. government performed? That is a general lead-in question. But then *within* that U.S. performance, what can we say about the performances chargeable to Congress specifically, or to the Congress-and-presidency interactions that characterize the U.S. separation-of-powers arrangement? As will be seen, this reach into peer comparisons also affords a method to choose policy realms to examine. Speculation and judgment bedeck this analysis throughout. But I believe there is payoff. Certainly we Americans keep making comparisons: There have been audiences for England envy, Sweden envy, the task of keeping up with China, and so on. As the United States has traveled through history in the world's pack, performances, whether we salute them in looking back at them or are today appalled by them, have been rendered. What have been the signature imprints of Congress in these performances?

1

Impulses and Imprints

I promised a complicated, roundabout way of proceeding. Here it is. Obviously, Congress is not the only federal institution that makes an imprint on American society and life. Even without considering the judicial system, which I ignore (no doubt at great cost), there is that other voter-based institution, the presidency. The presidency cannot be ignored.[1] My solution is to *partial out,* so to speak, the particular contribution that Congress makes to any imprint, taking into account the presidency. More on that below. But I want to make it clear upfront that, in considering each of various policy realms, I look square-on at the presidency as well as at Congress. I do this, though, in the service of *reaching past* the presidency to get a particular bead on Congress.

Yet I have another major moving part. I want to locate the performance of Congress in transnational perspective. This requires U.S. comparisons with peer countries. At stake at the end of analysis are such questions as: Has the U.S. welfare state, or the U.S. handling of deficits and debt, or American imperial expansion in the world, and so on, evolved in a distinctive way *because of the operations of Congress?* These are basic questions for any appraiser of the U.S. regime. Here is how I undertake the analysis. In each of a variety of realms, I ask first of all how the imprint of *the U.S. government system as a whole* has stacked up against those of peer countries; then, having done that,

I wrestle with partialing out the possibly distinct imprints of the presidency and Congress. Nightmarish problems of tractability attend this enterprise, but the questions are fundamental.

That is the setup. Now, what exactly is to be looked at? Choices need to be made. I go large. I aim for patches of performance that have entailed large considerations of regime legitimacy, order, responsiveness, welfare, prosperity, fairness, state-building, or national survival or expansion in an often hostile international world. I empiricize this quest in a particular way. I key on certain transnational, let us say, "impulses." I focus on U.S. participation in large political or intellectual impulses that have occurred transnationally during the relevant centuries since 1789. This resort to transnational focus has two uses. First, it guides the selection of realms of performance to look at. If something big is going on in a lot of countries at once, whatever it is may be especially worth taking a look at. Second, it paves the way to appraisals. It can offer clues to relative performance—the United States versus the rest—albeit not clues of a quality that would admit to score-keeping or quantification.

What is a transnational "impulse"? Consider the theorist Hegel, with his view of how world history proceeds. I draw on aspects of that view. This is perhaps an odd reliance in a study of American politics, but I find his insight about an evolving world "spirit" apt. Everywhere, in the view of Hegel, history rolls along, and as a poser of possibilities it does not respect borders. Transnational zeitgeists and contagions are in large supply. Think of nineteenth-century imperial expansion, late nineteenth-century socialism, the quest for economic growth, or the quest to control climate change. Consciousness evolves cross-nationally, as do economic and other kinds of situations, problems, norms, urges, and opportunities. Available in consequence, for analytic purposes, is a kind of transnational Hegelian yardstick.

Again, the analysis here is in principle empirical. "Impulses" make an appearance in history, and they are detectable. One can see what they are and how they are participated in. The roster of usual-suspect countries to compare the United States with evolves, as does history generally, but some such counterparts are always there.

There is a touch of Darwin here as well as Hegel. Nation-states that do not measure up can decline or get weeded out.

To proceed this way injects a stern dose of realism. It ignores the realm of political aspirations. It invites the "dismal science" tag that is sometimes applied to economics. In contrast, popular politics is a different kind of story. Politics, especially when considered at the level of popular or partisan ideologies, has much in common with religion. In practice, the goals of ideologies are never achieved fully and only raggedly achieved in part. Barriers of practical difficulty or of cause-and-effect impossibility intrude. All political platforms are at least partly utopian. My measurement and evaluative base here is *the real,* at least as it is tappable into by considering what has actually happened in a comparison base of countries, as opposed to *what is variously aspired to.* Aspirations, which as citizens we could hardly conduct political life without, are not my topic.

Let me ward off some possible misapprehensions. This is not exactly a survey of U.S. "problem solving." Some of the cases I consider have that cast—that is, they exhibit wide agreement on the fact of a problem, wide agreement on the goal, and an acknowledged pathway of intention and calculation that connects those dots at least in aim. But some of my cases do not have much of that cast. My yardstick is more like a historian's. In any case under scrutiny, as we look back at the history with a cold eye, peer into a jumble of aims and behaviors, what can we say about this country's arrival at an end-state that other countries have also tended to attain? That result occurs regardless of whether the routes to the end-states have entailed eyes-open problem solving or planning. What have been the impulses, and to what degree, using the posited transnational gauge, have they spurred action? Those are the operative questions.

As opposed to "impulses," I spent a good deal of time considering "challenges" as the guiding metaphor for this work. A society may be said to "participate in impulses." Yet alternatively, a society may be said to "respond to challenges." A reader of this book might substitute the latter phrase throughout without causing much harm or confusion. "Responding to challenges" fits pretty well many of the instances I take up. But others not so well. I shied away from "challenges." I decided that it smacked too much of problem solving and collective intentionality, not to mention teleology. The relevant history is sometimes more anarchic, disordered, turbulent, less fixed on any envisioned goal. I see "impulses" as a more comprehensive category. It accommodates the general case in which a patch of activity flashes up, occurs, and arrives at a common end-state in a variety of countries, including the United States, during a common time span.

There is a related caution: A rare sight in the cases I discuss is anything like decision by consensus. Machiavelli wrote that conflict, not consensus, is a trademark of republics, and that idea matches pretty well the American experience reported here.[2] The conflict has often been brutal. Consider obviously the Civil War of the 1860s.

Finally, there is the question of "progress." Is the cascade of U.S. performance since 1789 as I discuss it here a record of "progress," as seen in the Whig theory of history of nineteenth-century England?[3] Well, yes, in one way. That result is largely built into the method. Generally speaking, in this and other countries, successful arrival at a sequence of specified end-states is indeed what has happened. But this pattern should not be confused with any otherwise arrived-at verdict of "progress." Appraised differently, history might be seen as running into a ditch for the last two centuries. (To allow for such a ditch interpretation is to part ways with Hegel.) Looking back, it is a matter of normative judgment whether the impulses I take up here should have been bought into at all. At least one of them, continental expansion during the early nineteenth century, was indeed quite appalling. Whether "performances," as I used the term, were taking place is, in principle, independent of whether in casting our eyes back today we are delighted or appalled at what went on.

As stated earlier, I have relied on secondary sources for this enterprise. For transnational comparisons, I consult a representative scholarship, although my treatment is, generally speaking, stylized. This is an allowable course, I hope, given the largely well-known and non-controversial nature of the patterns. For the American history, I have tried to emphasize recent scholarship, which in many cases amends old interpretations. I reach beyond standard history and political science into especially economic history. As for which aspects of the history to look at, I emphasize policy over process. I key on the content of policies and the downstream effects of making them. This choice is at odds with most treatments of Congress in political science, which lean to elections and internal processes.

My accounts here may seem telegraphic. That is because, relying on what seem like authoritative sources, I often reach for the *gists* of causal stories about who did what and when and with what consequence. I leave behind the dynamics and the details. As recompense, I take pains to pinpoint the references to specified pages or at least chapters so that this work can be read as, among other things, a low-labor-costs bibliography. Often, these gists signal whether Congress or the presidency was chiefly responsible for something that happened.[4] It goes without saying that judgment calls on this question can falter. For one thing, theoretical intricacy can intrude—for example, one side may anticipate the other side's reactions. But common sense based on evidence seems a decent enough reliance. For my inferences of responsibility, I look for a balance of initiative, attention, energy, and muscle. Who was apparently generating what? But I should douse upfront the idea that this is a study of zero-sum relations between Congress and the presidency—one wins, the other loses. Sometimes that is the relation, but sometimes it is not. The thrusts and imprints of the two institutions may differ without being discordant one versus the other. They may just have different profiles and destinations. This is often the nature of coexistence between Congress and the executive branch.

In the following chapters, I address thirteen "impulses" of transnational resonance that the American governmental system can be said to have partaken of, reckoned with, or performed in accordance with starting in 1789 (see figure 1). This list is not exhaustive, it is selective, although it hits many orthodox high points. I aim for the major.

In the crosshairs here, I should make it clear, are performances by the U.S. federal government. I am not taking up activities or changes at the level of state or local government or ones that occur all the time more or less autonomously in the society or the economy. The list tilts toward the present—no doubt in part because the federal government grew more active during the twentieth century. The last two cases—handling environmental change and debts/deficits—probably belong in a category by themselves since the history on them is not finished. On "owl of Minerva" grounds familiar from Hegel—who knows how the history will happen?—I skirt a variety of other matters being discussed in the present day that may or may not come to enjoy primacy

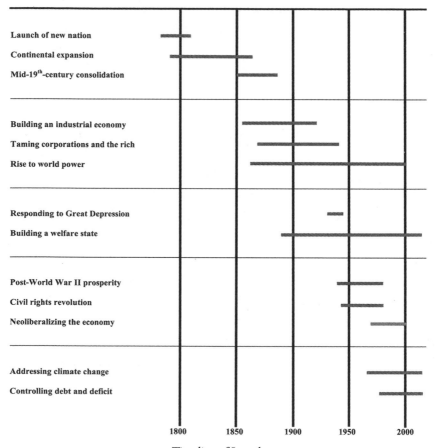

1. Timeline of Impulses.
Source: Prepared by John A. Dearborn.

and show sticking power. There are always itches and angsts, especially among intellectuals, but we cannot tell where they will go.

Again, I do not intend these thirteen instances to be exhaustive of U.S. history. Even so, as can be seen in figure 1, they do have a flavor of mapping the history. Insofar as they amount to that, the pattern of the mapping is unorthodox. That is intentional. I believe that the conventional periodizations of U.S. history have become rather stale. We have probably heard enough about the Jacksonian era, the New Deal era, the Reagan era, and the rest. Much recent scholarship has undermined or amended these periodizations. Aside from this, I believe that these old understandings have been too insular. In general, they haven't paid enough attention to transnational comparisons, which can be illuminating. Also, they haven't centered enough on actual U.S. policy regimes and their impacts. Relatedly, I steer clear here of the aspirations, the teleologies, and the celebratory back-patting claims associated with the American political parties. Those propensities are well known and have been dwelt on often. The parties do figure here, but I emphasize the activities of individuals and formal institutions.

I take up the impulses in a series of sketches. Following the design of figure 1, I sort the thirteen sketches into five chapters. This grouping is more or less chronological, but with considerable imperfection. The imperfection owes to the waywardness of the real history. I accommodate the sprawls of varying location, epicenter, and length that the various policy or performance regimes have traveled. I start each of the thirteen sketches with a discussion of the policy performance of the United States placed in transnational perspective. But each such discussion is in principle a preparation for, and is followed by, a consideration of the particular roles of the U.S. executive branch and, especially, Congress in the rendition of a particular imprint. Again, this setup is meant as an entryway into Congress. To get a fix on Congress, we need to know what the impulses have been, how the United States has fared against the transnational field—perhaps Congress has veered the result one way or another—and the roles of the American executive branch as well as Congress.

2

Building a State and a Nation

My account begins in 1789, when the United States, having ratified its new Constitution, kick-started its new Congress, presidency,
and courts. That means I miss an earlier transnational "impulse" of
great importance. An "age of the democratic revolution," it has been
argued, began with the U.S. Declaration of Independence of 1776,
invested France and the rest of Europe, and extended through most of
the Western Hemisphere during the succeeding decades.[1]

But the late eighteenth century was early in this sequence, and
it was far from clear what a new, ex-colonial, intentionally crafted
nation could amount to. Beyond that, in those days of slow and
chancy communications and transportation and generally weak instruments of central government, it was not clear how the traditional
political units of Europe would evolve, either. Much was to happen
everywhere.

By today's standards the United States at its outset was radically
something else. It was a precarious rim on a large continent. It was
a slave empire, in large part. It was a decentralized sprawl. It has
been called a "states-union," as distinct from a conventional, run-
from-the-center national state.[2] It could have faltered or fallen apart.
In world history, many are the political units that might have become
viable national states but did not make it.[3] In this chapter, I take
up three U.S. performances along the way to the successful national

consolidation that did come about in the 1860s. Placed in perspective, what was the role of Congress?

Launching the New Nation

A launch is topic number one. It is not easy to launch a new polity that works and lasts. For the new United States, the best peer comparisons are probably the new Latin American republics after 1800 or the British settler polities that came into being somewhat later—Canada, Australia, and New Zealand. Matched against these nations, the United States developed quite well. It became more stable and prosperous and better anchored in legitimacy than the Latin American republics (of course, problems of comparison arise) and at least the equal of the British colonies in economic growth.[4] One economic assessment goes: "The faster growth of the early United States in comparison to the growth of its northern and southern neighbors and other 'new' countries suggests that U.S. policies launched in the 1790s did make a difference in relative economic performance."[5] This is to approach the new polities as they were constituted: The United States, like the British units but unlike many of the Latin American ones as they evolved into independence, was whites-only in effective membership.[6]

How about the institutions of the new U.S. government? Unquestionably, the economic success of the new republic was executive-led. Backed up by George Washington's steadiness and charisma,[7] Alexander Hamilton, the Treasury secretary, acted as something like a prime minister. He nourished into existence a funded debt, the Bank of the United States, the Customs Service, the Coast Guard (smugglers had to be warded off so as to allow collection of imposts at the ports), the U.S. Mint, a bustling securities market, readmission to the British trading area, and, indirectly, the New York Stock Exchange.

It was quite a performance. There is a wealth of recent research on these subjects.[8] Hamilton is said to have been "the first systematic macroeconomic planner in the United States and one of the first in any country."[9] Courtesy of Hamilton, the United States was "one of the first nations [after the Netherlands and Britain] to modernize its finances."[10] The results seem to have been decisive—low taxes, an explosion of entrepreneurialism, and "history's most successful emerging market."[11] In short order, the mid-1790s brought an "increasing growth of American prosperity. Hamilton's financial program was working wonders."[12] A long economic growth surge began. In one assessment, the policy choices of the 1790s "not only established conditions for (and removed constraints on) modern economic growth, but also provided a long-term policy framework that continued to encourage growth, the territorial expansion of the United States, and the country's influence on world affairs for decades and centuries."[13]

Absent Hamilton and his policies, what? Well, to reach for an extreme, one plausible counter-scenario would see the new nation as an agricultural backwater beset by debt, taxes, low growth, centrifugal forces, Indian tribes, the Spanish and the British, and, if commercial development were to falter (as it likely would), mired even deeper in southern slavery than the country in fact came to be.[14] The agrarian-minded Jeffersonian Republicans who took over the national government in 1801, skeptical of commercialism though they might have been, were lucky to inherit a thriving fiscal system and economy, not to mention a good navy (which they proceeded to use in North Africa in the "Barbary Wars").[15] In terms of historiography, our last few decades have belonged to Hamilton. Popular culture has followed. We have a Broadway show called *Hamilton*, but I have not heard of one called *Jefferson* or *Madison*.

This was the executive side. But there was a congressional role, too. It is as legitimizer of the system in the eyes of U.S. citizens. That theme will echo in this book. As many of us learned in school, to cite a particular, the ratification of the Constitution was accompanied by a certain nervousness, especially among the anti-Federalists, about not having a bill of rights. In response, the Bill of Rights as we know it was quickly written and ratified. It issued from the House of Representatives in 1789 thanks to James Madison, then the chamber's leading member.[16]

A stable system needs a way to channel opposition to its executive. The parties emerged as one American solution, but Congress emerged as another—often as a venue for the parties. Given the Constitution's design, power-checking, not just expressiveness, could figure grandly in congressional opposition. Finances were an early source of contention. In the mid-1790s, the House created a Ways and Means Committee "so that Congress could counter the [financial] expertise and experience that until that time had been monopolized by the executive branch."[17] This was a significant move in power-checking, a likely assistance to legitimizing the system in both the short and long term. The congressional committee system was being born. Albert Gallatin, the era's talented intellectual adversary to Hamilton on financial questions, found a footing in the Ways and Means Committee and the House of Representatives in general as that chamber came to harbor an anti-Federalist opposition.[18]

Foreign policy was another hot spot. The era's wrangling over banking and credit once preoccupied historians, but lately foreign policy has surged in attention. For one thing, we have come to appreciate the importance of U.S. reentry into the British trading area. That access had been lost thanks to national independence. Nothing in the 1790s seems to have topped the drama and conflict attending a key step in that reentry, which Congress finalized in approving the Washington administration's Jay Treaty in 1795–96, a deal with Britain that covered trade and other controversial matters. As with the era's banking and credit policies, the Federalists triumphed over congressional Republicans of a Jeffersonian/Madisonian persuasion (who were also confusingly called Democratic-Republicans, and eventually just Democrats). There are several excellent accounts of the enactment process. The Senate approved the Jay Treaty by a two-thirds vote, but a follow-up House assent was needed to implement it. The crunch came on the House of Representatives side. For the country, it brought an education in the channeling of contestation. In that respect, it set precedents. It featured eight months of tense conflict accompanied by mobilization of interests and voters on both sides plus shifts in public opinion that ended in a House majority party being "rolled," to use a term of today's political science, by a winning cross-party coalition.[19] The parties could be players, it turned out, but so could public opinion. The House's party alignment statistics are cloudy for those early days, but it seems proper to denominate the Republicans the chamber's majority party as of the spring of 1796, the Federalists the minority. "With a strong Republican majority in Congress, the treaty opponents were easy winners on [several procedural] votes, and the treaty appeared doomed. But on the final two votes, Republican unity broke down and the treaty won narrowly."[20] This was a lesson in how to lose: The crushed Madisonians were not history's last losers to find that a roll call loss rooted in public opinion is basically unspinnable. Life has to go on.

Finally, in 1801 a House controlled by a Federalist majority now fallen to lame-duck status managed to award the presidency to Thomas Jefferson in the tense election settlement of that year. The election of 1800 had ended in an Electoral College mess, and under the Constitution the lame-duck House of Representatives had the deciding power. (Technically, in a confusing ingredient that I won't dwell on here, the choice in the House came down to Republican Party leader Jefferson versus his edgy co-partisan running mate Aaron Burr. The Federalists toyed with Burr as a possible monkey wrench.) After a tense deadlock, certain Federalists in the chamber prone to compromise joined a cross-party coalition in a nod to the widely understood national voter verdict for Jefferson, thus breaking a stalemate and doing the trick.[21] Jefferson went to the White House. One recent judgment goes: "The constitutional miracle, if there was one, did not happen in the Philadelphia of 1787 but in the Washington of 1801. It is one thing to write a Constitution, quite another for it to survive. . . ."[22] In comparative terms, this American party turnover of 1801 was a significant first.[23] Democracy, in Adam Przeworski's influential definition, is "a system in which parties lose elections."[24] For us today, it may be a dog-bites-man story that a party in presidential power for twelve years freshly encumbered by a war scare entailing heavy, unpopular taxes and a security clampdown, as were the Federalists thanks to this country's now largely forgotten "quasi-war" versus France in the late 1790s, can lose an election.[25] In one estimate, the Jeffersonian Republicans won a telling 52 percent of the nationwide popular vote across a variety of sub-presidential offices in 1800 (a usable popular vote result for president does not exist).[26] But going into 1800, an election-induced government turnover had never happened. Congress was the site of settlement.

All these congressional instances map onto the idea of Congress-induced legitimization. Certainly the executive-centered Federalists with their humming economy were system-legitimizers, too. But politically, the Federalists could be all thumbs. Note that this discussion of legitimizing points up a framing argument I made earlier.

True, many political actors of the first-generation 1790s were notably open-eyed about setting good institutional precedents. So it is documented.[27] But it would be odd to say that the congressional actors discussed above were trying in an intentional sense to "solve the problem" of "launching the new nation" by "legitimizing" it. That seems like a claim too far. Rather, their assortment of behavior, however it was animated or intended, much of it being in fact scrappily partisan, can be reasonably judged to have contributed to an arrival at a particular end-state—a successful launch.

Continental Expansion

On to performance number two. The new country soon rushed beyond an eastern continental rim. It rushed south and southwest as well as west. A wholly new continental rim accrued along the Gulf of Mexico.

As a nineteenth-century expansion power, the United States was one of a pack. Peoples of European ancestry invaded, seized, and settled vast terrain outside Europe, thus displacing or exterminating native populations as they did so. No impulse was more common. Five continents were involved. Siberia, South Africa, and the South American cone countries of Chile and Argentina were among the expansion zones, yet the cleanest analogy to America's drive to the south and west may be the British settler colonies of Canada, Australia, and New Zealand. Millions of settlers flocked to those inviting spaces, too.[28]

I accent here the first half or so of the nineteenth century, although the impulse continued on: The U.S. Indian wars after the 1860s, for example, had a clear counterpart in Argentina.[29] As an exercise of ethnic cleansing, this country's "Indian removal" of the

Jacksonian 1830s had an especially clear, indeed an eerie, parallel in Australia's Tasmania and New South Wales at the exact same time.[30] In all the five continents, the nineteenth-century expansions, looked at in their own terms, were certainly successful. No U.S. anomaly there. Otherwise, in brutality toward the native populations the Americans and Australians apparently outdid the Canadians.[31] Probably the chief respect in which the Americans stood out was in their need to shunt aside established national powers—Britain, France, Spain, and eventually Mexico, not just indigenous peoples—in order to seize the geographic spaces they sought to occupy.

White settler pressure paced it all. But in the United States the federal government played a prime role—not least to usher out those other established powers. That ordinarily meant leadership by the executive branch. An exception was the War of 1812, a drive for territory, among other things, where Congress nudged the action.[32] But Congress ordinarily just followed along and complied, occasionally complaining or constraining. There is no doubt that the White House ordinarily supplied the initiative and energy. The presidents used a variety of acquisition techniques. One was purchases: Thomas Jefferson bought the huge Louisiana territory from France in 1803; the Franklin Pierce administration engineered the Gadsden Purchase—a last swath along the southern borders of today's New Mexico and Arizona—from Mexico in 1853; Secretary of State William Seward bought Alaska (acting for President Andrew Johnson in the last acquisition on the North American continent) from Russia in 1867.[33] There was annexation: President John Tyler set the process to acquire Texas that way in 1845.[34] There was invasion: President James K. Polk acquired half the land area of Mexico that way in 1846–48 (he would have taken more, but, among other things, Congress was hostile).[35] Along the Gulf Coast from today's Florida into Louisiana—a thousand-mile strip then called, confusingly for us today, "the Floridas"—possessed at the time by Indian tribes and the Spanish, Presidents James Madison and James Monroe engineered, presided over, or gave a wink and a nod to a mix of techniques that in today's terms seem positively Putinesque. Secret schemes, armed intrusions, rampages, and forced treaties abounded.[36] For a map of these various expansions to the south and southwest, see figure 2.

As for the removal of Native Americans to the West, it was envisioned by, among others, Jefferson, but it took on reality in the long career of Andrew Jackson as general and president.[37] For Jackson, once in the White House, according to one recent account, "The

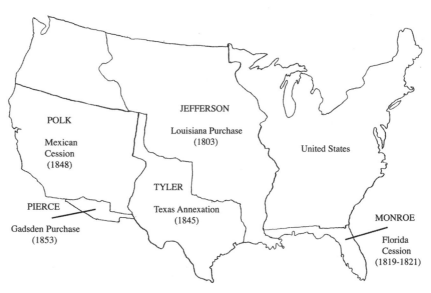

2. U.S. Territorial Expansions to the South and Southwest, 1800–1860.
Source: Prepared by John A. Dearborn.

Indian Removal Act of 1830 constituted the highest priority in the new president's legislative agenda."[38] Then he sped past the terms of congressional authorization in implementing it.[39]

What was Jacksonian democracy? In Daniel Walker Howe's recent uncomplimentary take, "In the first place it was about the extension of white supremacy across the North American continent."[40] These days, the portraits of both Jefferson and Jackson are being turned to the wall. The Democrats are abandoning their vintage Jefferson-Jackson Day dinners.[41] There is too much back there about slavery and ethnic cleansing.

But even in its customary whites-only meaning, I have sidestepped casting "Jacksonian democracy" as a free-standing "impulse" category in this study. A decent cross-country comparison doesn't seem on offer. Also, the expansion of American democracy came chiefly at the state and local, not national, levels. But most important, the Jacksonian connection to democracy has sagged in recent scholarship. In fact, U.S. voter participation seems to have surged earlier in time, not particularly in the 1830s, at least for sub-presidential elections—not a bad place to look into in a quite decentralized system.[42] New data collected by Philip Lampi "confirm the huge expansion of popular participation within two decades or so of the adoption of the United States Constitution." Also, "This expansion was possible because the right to vote had always been extraordinarily widespread— at least among adult white males [even before U.S. independence]."[43] All in all, the idea of assigning a special democratic stamp to the Jacksonian 1830s has not been faring well.

The executive branch led in acquiring the vast new public land. But Congress led in distributing it. There is no doubt about the latter. The system's rules needed setting, and Congress set them. The dominant role of Congress pervades the sources, although Albert Gallatin as Treasury secretary was an impressive administrator of it all from 1801 to 1813.[44] I resorted to an old, not a recent, scholarship for this story, and a fine scholarship it was and remains. Not much seems to have been written recently.[45] The politics is fascinating. Anyone devoted to congressional history should be aware of it.

The story begins with an unlikelihood for a legislative body. In the pre-Constitution mid-1780s, the Continental Congress (the predecessor to the Congress we are familiar with) generated through its committee processes one of the world's most rationalistic master plans. Thomas Jefferson had a hand in it. It was synoptic planning at a maximum—a long-odds outcome for a committee. The whole U.S. public domain was assigned into small rectangles for purposes of surveying and sales.[46] That geographic design stuck. It made for a famous map. Certain fundamental premises stuck, also. Land was to go out to the public, not kept by the government. It was to be commodified—that is, made freely buyable and sellable—a contrast to practices in much of continental Europe. It was to be made ownable in fairly small packets—a contrast to much of Europe and Latin America. Governments, state as well as federal, would preside over the land sales.

But this rationalistic planning by a legislative body came upfront. After that, in stylistic contrast, seven decades of trademark congressional politics took over. It is a revealing saga. It is a wonder that any incumbent politician ever lost an election. They all had a continent of land to hand out! In the enactment of hundreds of congressional laws—yes, hundreds, it was virtually nonstop—from the 1790s into the 1860s, here were the themes: Cater to land speculators as well as aspiring farmers, keep lowering the sales prices (eventually to zero), keep allowing ever smaller land plots, allow easy credit for purchases, supply debt relief once the farmers' debt builds up, legalize the claims of the inevitable squatters on vacant land, accommodate the war veterans (land plots were the pre–Civil War version of veterans' benefits), don't worry about the government making money from distributing the land, and keep changing the rules.[47] It was a ragged, volatile legislative populism.

Some of the executive branch's leaders regretted not taking in more revenue from the sales (Treasury secretaries Hamilton and Gallatin) or blanched at the accommodation of the squatters (Gallatin and Jackson) or at the easy credit (Jackson—whose controversial Specie Circular of 1836 requiring land payments in gold and silver took aim at it).[48] Note that these executives were from both parties— Hamilton the Federalist, Gallatin and Jackson the Democratic-Republican and Democrat. In the end, the federal government seems to have broken even, more or less—there was no windfall of revenue but also no loss.[49] The consequences of it all? A nation of small farmers was speedily helped into existence—notwithstanding the rampant land speculation, although much of the South's land taken from Indians did end up in slave plantations. Perhaps, according to one account by economists, the quick move of the land into production assisted the U.S. economic growth rate.[50]

There is a final division of labor. Many vast holdings of public land have never been given out or sold. The presidency, in a stream of executive directives originating in the 1790s and lasting through today, has decisively shaped the *management* of those lands remaining in government possession. By way of such directives has public land often been reserved or tailored for Indian tribes, military use, environmental preservation, and so on—and sometimes curbed from sale. Across all policy areas, little in the history of executive directives has been more important.[51]

National Consolidation

Generally speaking, the mid-nineteenth century, notably the 1860s, seems to have brought a spasm of special character across much of the developed or developing world. Upended were old particularisms like church privileges, monasteries, autarkic principalities, rebellious regions, corporate orders, serfdom, feudal land rights, and slavery. Centralizing states swung into place offering strong nationalisms, new constitutional formulas, a spirit of reform in state and economy, and a bent for commodifying property and homogenizing the rights of citizenship across entire populations.[52] If an identifying tag is needed, "modernizing liberalism" in the nineteenth-century usage of the latter term is probably as good as any. Among other things, although I have not seen a convincing discussion of mechanism, dramatic midcentury changes in transportation and communication were possibly a key to the era's profile.[53]

Partaking of this apparent 1860s spasm in varying respects were at least Germany, Italy, Austria and Hungary, Japan, Mexico, Argentina—and the United States.[54] Not so much Britain and France, where many of the developments discussed here were already in place—although Britain did expand its voter franchise in 1867. Among the particulars, Russia emancipated its serfs in 1861, the United States its slave population in 1863 and 1865, the Austro-Hungarian Habsburg realm its Jewish population in 1867, Germany its Jewish population in 1869 and 1871.[55]

Historians often rope the United States into comparisons.[56] Thus E. J. Hobsbawm: "For one reason or another three types of agrarian enterprise were under particular pressure: the slave plantation, the serf estate, and the traditional non-capitalist peasant economy. The first was liquidated in the United States and most parts of Latin America. . . . The second was formally liquidated in Europe between 1848 and 1969. . . ."[57] C. A. Bayly: "In crushing the emergent Confederate state, the Union was itself following, and contributing to, a much wider realignment in which large and unified nations and more centralized and economically sophisticated supremacies replaced the still loose and varied polities of the early nineteenth century."[58] Peter Kolchin takes up "this American emancipation of the 1860s in comparative context, paying particular attention to the other emancipation of the 1860s—that of the Russian serfs."[59] For its part, the United States is said to have "entered [the Civil War] a states-union in crisis and emerged from it a federal state and with a strengthened liberal-democratic national identity."[60] The country's slavery went out. Expanded citizenship rights, a "free labor" ideology, and "an explosive expansion of central state authority" came in.[61] (I emphasize here the rights, identity, and national sovereignty aspects of these changes; for the economic side, see chapter 3.)

In these respects, the 1860s seem to have brought a transnational ideological high. Ensuing years brought a recession from it—in at least Germany, Austria, Russia, Mexico, and the United States—as the promises and commitments of the decade wore down. In this country, the thrusts of rights expansion lost force in the 1870s.[62]

Unquestionably, the American change of the 1860s was executive-led. In the United States as in most other countries mentioned above, wars figured in the consolidations.[63] There was an executive edge of force and steel. Abraham Lincoln as president is sometimes compared to other violence-ready national consolidators of that era, Germany's Otto von Bismarck and Italy's Count Cavour, or even to the later V. I. Lenin of Russia's civil war of 1918–21.[64] In Lincoln there is also a flavor of Simón Bolívar of the earlier Latin American wars for independence if, as is emphasized in recent scholarship, winning the American Civil

War required a mobilization of the U.S. enslaved population into the Union army and, as a consequence, into political life.[65]

What was the place of Congress in this history? During the Civil War itself, with the South now seceded and absent, Congress sluiced into a subsidiary and generally cooperative role vis-à-vis Lincoln—at least in matters related to war management.[66] Enough said. Looking back at the era more broadly, and theoretically, one way to interpret it is as a trade-off between direct and virtual representation. Congress is ordinarily good at representing *directly* the views of the American voting population. Before the 1860s, that meant white (male) voters of the North and the South. As of 1860, the country's African Americans, almost all enslaved, were a seventh of the total population, and nearly none could vote. As our school textbooks told us, Congress in the decades running up to 1860 spent a great deal of time and energy making North-versus-South deals—the Missouri Compromise, the Compromise of 1850, and so on. No Capitol Hill activity was more prominent. Henry Clay, Daniel Webster, Stephen Douglas, and other members of Congress earned acclaim through oratorical force and procedural inventiveness in the task of keeping the Union together.[67] In doing so, they were preserving or updating the legitimacy of the system among white voters across the regions. Both Massachusetts and South Carolina needed to be appeased. Perhaps conflict over slavery could be bridged or at least postponed. The nation's median voter likely resided at this nexus of those deals during those times. Right into the secession crisis in the winter of 1860–61, Congress's instinct was to make another deal. It was representing the voters.

In contrast, the role of the victorious Lincoln Republicans of 1860 has a flavor of *virtual* representation—that is, in theory, someone taking steps to represent in the government an interest excluded from formal suffrage ties. In 1860, the Republicans, a party winning with Lincoln 39.9 percent of the total national presidential vote in a four-party race, poised at an antislavery extreme on the country's slavery-antislavery dimension, captured the White House thanks to the Electoral College.[68] No Electoral College, no Lincoln presidency. African Americans could be represented, in a sense, in this way. In the pre–Civil War decades, Congresses had had a hand in virtual representation, too. The processes of Capitol Hill offered a speaking platform. Certain members famously used it, thus drawing an audience and apparently radiating influence across the country. This was position taking with consequence. John Quincy Adams fought to admit antislavery petitions. David Wilmot pressed his post–Mexican War "proviso" to keep slavery from the annexed new territories. Charles Sumner delivered and sent around the country his antislavery speeches, drawing a physical assault on the Senate floor for doing so.[69]

Once the Civil War was over, Congress kept true to its custom of accommodating the median voter, whoever that median voter might be. In the Reconstruction Congresses of the late 1860s, the southern states that had abandoned the national legislature during the war were kept unrepresented. For a brief time, the median national voter underpinning congressional elections was, say, a Pennsylvanian in the North, not a Kentuckian in the border states. Probably the median northerner also bought into the era's ideological cause. But then the white South came back to Capitol Hill,[70] the voting rights of the South's African Americans fell away through violence and casuistry, and Congress's antebellum practice of bridging the interests of whites across the sections resumed—this time entailing coalitional and procedural wrinkles that I will take up in chapter 7. A southern racial caste system hardened into place.

3

Surges and Their Constraints

After Appomattox, the close of the Civil War in 1865, the gloves were off. The American industrial economy was poised to burst forth, as was the American national state as a player in the world's affairs. The newly muscular states of Germany and Japan, also products of that era, joining a mix with Britain and France, were to exhibit similar trajectories. In this chapter, with a particular eye for Congress, I take up three American "impulses" of post–Civil War times. They entail both domestic and foreign policy. I consider relevant American surges as well as reactions to, or constraints on, those surges. The dating of the impulses is untidy. (See figure 1.) One of the timelines goes on until recent days.

Building an Industrial Economy

Generally speaking, political scientists writing about American history see it as a story of zero-sum politics. Two sides, the progressives versus the conservatives or some such pairing of antagonists, occasionally more than two sides, slug it out. We see that pattern, for example, in the congressional roll call history.[1] Yet looked at differently, the two-century record is one of positive-sum economics. Economic growth raises all, or at least most, boats. Across two centuries the boats could get immensely lofted. But that does not happen innocent of government. Obviously, as witness Alexander Hamilton, the actions of government can figure in the positive-sum sphere as well as the zero-sum sphere. Just how they might figure is an empirical matter. But they figure. Hence, a study like this should be alert to transnational zooms in economic performance, sometimes exhibiting a nation-versus-nation competitive animation, and to whatever jumps out in the way of governmental fostering of them. "Impulses" of a sort come into focus.

Thus the United States during and after the Civil War. One summary judgment goes: "Destructive though it was, the Civil War broke the slaveocracy's power to obstruct an American development agenda."[2] Economic improvement took on new life with an often rivalrous eye on especially Britain and, later, a burgeoning Germany. It was a race to the top. During the war itself in the 1860s, "one of the great development programs in American history" was entered into. An old Whig policy mix became politically feasible in updated design once the South seceded from the Union and the Republicans rose to power. On the books went the Morrill Tariff of 1861 (much steeper rates on imports), the Homestead Act of 1862 (this time, land for western settlers at no purchase cost), the Morrill Land-Grant College Act of 1862 (land subsidies to generate agricultural and industrial colleges for training and research),[3] and the Pacific Railroad Act of 1862 (public land subsidies for a transcontinental line to the West Coast). To witness the jolt upward in the tariff, a map of the new colleges (including those from a follow-up enactment in 1890), and a map of the new transcontinental railroad, see figures 3, 4, and 5. All this added up to an economic development program. The Land-Grant College Act, for example, has been seen as "one of the most fundamental interventions by the federal government in the process of economic growth."[4] The American government was not alone in these assertions. Next door, the Canadian government advanced a similar program of high tariffs, a transcontinental railway, and western settlement in the 1870s.[5]

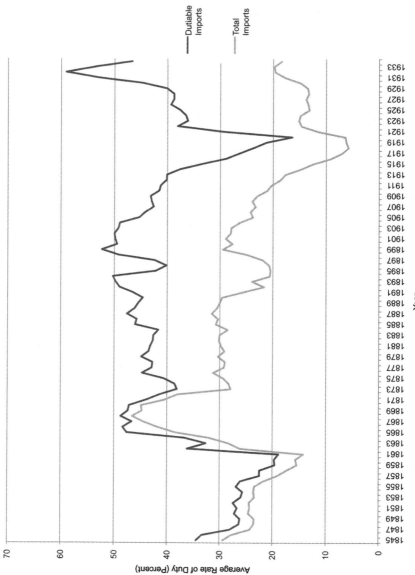

Dutiable Imports

Total Imports

Year

Average Rate of Duty (Percent)

70

60

50

40

30

20

10

0

1845 1847 1849 1851 1853 1855 1857 1859 1861 1863 1865 1867 1869 1871 1873 1875 1877 1879 1881 1883 1885 1887 1889 1891 1893 1895 1897 1899 1901 1903 1905 1907 1909 1911 1913 1915 1917 1919 1921 1923 1925 1927 1929 1931 1933

4. Locations of the 1862 *and* 1890 *Land Grant Colleges and Universities.*
Source: Map from Committee on the Future of the Colleges of Agriculture in the Land Grant
System, Board of Agriculture, and National Research Council, *Colleges of Agriculture at the
Land Grant Universities: A Profile* (Washington, DC: National Academies Press, 1995), p. 8,
available at www.nap.edu/read/4980/chapter/2#8. Reprinted with permission from the
National Academies Press, copyright © 1995, National Academy of Sciences.

In general, this American program was congressional, not presidential. Managing the war was one thing, and Abraham Lincoln did press Congress on slavery—famously in generating the Thirteenth Amendment to abolish slavery. But otherwise, "Less than any other major American President did Lincoln control or even influence the

3. Average Rates of Duty for All Imports and for Dutiable Imports, 1845–1934.
Prepared by John A. Dearborn.
Source: Douglas A. Irwin, "Merchandise Imports and Duties: 1790–2000," Table Ee424–430
in Susan B. Carter et al. (eds.), *Historical Statistics of the United States, Earliest Times to the
Present: Millennial Edition* (New York: Cambridge University Press, 2006), available at http://
hsus.cambridge.org/HSUSWeb/toc/tableToc.do?id=Ee424–430.

5. *The First Transcontinental Railroad in 1869. Railroad joined from East and West at Promontory Summit, Utah, on May 10, 1869.*
Source: Figure 1 in Anan S. Raymond and Richard E. Fike, "Introduction," *Rails East to Promontory: The Utah Stations* (Salt Lake City: Bureau of Land Management, 1981). Originally in Robert M. Utley, *Promontory Summit,* The National Survey of Historic Sites and Buildings (National Park Service, Region 3, Santa Fe, New Mexico: U.S. Department of the Interior), available at www.nps.gov/parkhistory/online_books/blm/ut/8/intro.htm.

Congress. . . . The President had remarkably little connection with the legislation passed during the Civil War." The tariff, the homesteads, the railroad, the college funding, and other moves "had little connection with Lincoln aside from his formal approval of them."[6] Lincoln was not the only executive official. In institutional terms, the banking and currency domain had more of a joint flavor as Treasury Secretary Salmon P. Chase busily managed his department's policies and took part in a back-and-forth relation with Congress. Out of it all came a jointly remade banking system.[7] Yet in the financing of the Civil War itself, a recent account goes: "Congress rather than the Treasury secretary took the lead in fiscal legislation." Greenback currency, an income tax (which was allowed to lapse after the war ended), and a new internal revenue bureaucracy (which lasted) were congressional concoctions.[8]

U.S. industrial development certainly did take place. The record is striking. The decade of the 1870s brought a remarkable annual growth rate of 6.2 percent, a total output surge of 67 percent.[9] U.S. per capita income nearly tripled between 1870 and 1910.[10] Output came to outpace that of Britain, France, and Germany combined by 1914.[11]

Moves in the private economy offer plenty of causal grounding for these trends.[12] But how about the government, and how about Congress in particular, in the policymaking not only during the Civil War but in the decades after that? The pattern that accrues in various accounts is of a late nineteenth-century division of labor.[13] The federal courts came to guard private property rights and, parrying regulatory moves by the state governments, the workings of interstate markets.[14] The executive put down contagious railroad strikes (in 1877 and 1894), sometimes helped to manage currency crises (in 1893–94 and 1907), and protected the gold standard.[15] "The only factor that prevented the United States from switching from gold to silver or paper currency as the monetary standard was the unflinching position of the executive branch."[16] At the presidential level, Democratic as well as Republican leaders, notably the Democratic presidential nominees Samuel Tilden and Grover Cleveland, favored hard currency. Congress, for its part, pursued distributive politics—that is, the conferring of sectoral or individual benefits—as in the 1860s land subsidies—and leaned toward inflation that favored farmers and the silver industry—the latter a small-state interest well represented in the Senate.[17] "Congress was at best indifferent toward the maintenance of the gold standard and often outright hostile."[18]

And Congress kept the protective tariff high.[19] Legislators can be deft at logrolling and ladling out benefits, a premium skill in foreign trade politics. For political scientists, the analytic window into the tariff system of earlier times may still be E. E. Schattschneider's work of 1935 illuminating a practice of "reciprocal noninterference" among petitioners for tariff duties, which transmuted "a dubious economic policy . . . into a great political success."[20] It was a classic distributive coalitional politics. In the familiar reformers' critique, it overproduced import duties that mis-served the interests of the median voter as well as the economy's overall efficiency and, in terms of product by product, was distastefully ad hoc. This old reform interpretation likely has force, the logic is there, although new accounts have appeared. Overall, the tariff of earlier times seems to have had three animations. It was a U.S. policy antidote to Britain's dominance in international trade.[21] It was a principled neo-mercantilist program that the Republican Party pursued for, among other things, revenue reasons.[22] And it was the distributive Christmas tree enterprise that Schattschneider saw it as. Economists are still puzzling about its actual economic effects.[23] Interestingly, the traditional tariff was often carried by narrow congressional majorities; obstruction through congressional filibustering figured little in its fortunes.[24] At any rate, Congress in this old tariff system, as opposed to the White House, ordinarily dominated the process and favored higher rates.[25] Across history, presidents have leaned more toward free trade— ordinarily vis-à-vis at least their own congressional parties before 1932, uniformly vis-à-vis Congress as a whole regardless of party configurations since that time, at least through the Obama presidency.[26]

I came out of a literature search into this post–Civil War era with a reflection. On the side of government process, the scholarship seems rather stale and underdeveloped. Gilded Age stories of "a swinish scramble for government largesse," not that they lack a basis, have probably enjoyed too much resonance for too long.[27] An image comes down of the government being not only corrupt but also passive or asleep—a blank tablet on which private interests, often greedy ones, wrote. But was that really all? There is little analysis of government steering. We could use some better empirical investigation of the elite processes of those days—an alertness to evidence of design, of thought and behavior by government actors aimed at fostering a successful political economy. What is lurking in the documents? This kind of scholarship has been done for other eras. Here is an idea. A project centering on Ohio Republican senator and cabinet member John Sherman, who figured in economic policymaking in both Congress and the executive branch from the 1850s into the 1890s, would be a welcome addition to works like those on Alexander Hamilton's developmental role, on Henry Clay's prodding of an "American system" in antebellum times, or on Senator Robert F. Wagner's role in crafting the American welfare state in the 1930s.[28] Such a project could clarify the roles of Congress and the executive. Sherman's own two-volume account of his aims and actions, not a bedtime read but still available for purchase, is a four-decade-long story of policy steering. Both Congress and the executive had hands on the wheel in those days before the Federal Reserve System. In Sherman's account, Congress and the Treasury Department shared the unending task of stabilizing the U.S. currency between undue contraction or expansion, with the gold standard, then the international norm, as a leading device.[29] For better or worse—a matter of judgment then and since—that was the program.[30] In its favor, among other things, the stability of the gold standard was thought to supply a path for European investment in the United States—a welcome plus for, among others, farmers.[31] One current assessment of the old silver-versus-gold question of the late nineteenth century pulls no punches: "For historians intent on rehabilitating the late nineteenth century's many movements for currency reform, silverite ignorance of finance represents a major obstacle."[32]

Taming the Corporations and the Rich

If the "explosive economic growth" of late nineteenth-century America was singular,[33] so was the resulting social and political environment. The world's largest corporations, along with their creativity, their efficiencies, and their producer and consumer miracles like the railroads brought a whirlwind of disruptive change.[34] The picture is familiar. Market change intruded everywhere. Sweatshops grew. Booming Great Lakes industries drew vast immigration from Europe. Nationwide strikes kept breaking out. A new gaudy American plutocracy flexed its political muscles. No one had seen anything quite like it.

An understandable uneasiness set in and took political form. It is not exactly clear where to look for comparisons—in a general sense the European socialist movements, also British Liberalism around 1900, but the American path was distinctive.[35] By the late 1880s, a "pervasive antitrust sentiment" seems to have invited a public reckoning with the giant new U.S. corporations, notably the railroads.[36] A powerful "antimonopoly" coalition erupted into politics bent on achieving economic justice. It stretched across the two major parties and spurred third parties, notably the Populists of the 1890s. It voiced farmer interests and also had a labor component.[37] For an apt instance elsewhere of this brand of mobilization, at least in its pre-1900 phase centering on farmers, an especially good bet might be agricultural New Zealand of the late nineteenth century.[38] The American farm sector had gained economically over the years, but the farmers were suffering from market volatility and deflation.[39] After 1900, the American reform spirit morphed into Progressivism.

This late nineteenth-century antimonopolist impulse helped to trigger a striking and long-lasting American policy regime of business regulation and progressive taxation. I say "helped to trigger" because the causation was complex and multiple and there has been no end to interpreting it.[40] The antimonopoly spirit was at least a proximate and a necessary cause of it all. In came the independent regulatory agencies to order and police industries—an American specialty. The United States "was unique in relying on regulatory agencies," which "accrued autonomous power and applied rules in a legalistic manner unseen in any other country. . . . They are the American version of the Weberian bureaucratic state."[41] A "stringent policy against cartels," a regulatory bent dating to those times, is "a peculiarly American phenomenon."[42] American initiatives in progressive taxation of personal and corporate income topped off with gift and estate taxes seem to have paced the world, or at least tied for that distinction, a century ago. The U.S. revenue package then was a good deal more progressive than those of France and Sweden. Britain is a closer call.[43] "[V]ery high taxes on the very rich," Thomas Piketty writes, was a practice "invented in the United States."[44] Using the tax hammer, the era's reformers assaulted the country's new corporate wealth with a ferocity that is rarely seen today.[45] The take-them-down-a-peg script continued into the 1930s.[46]

This regulate-and-tax regime was dominantly congressional. In general, Congress did the initiating and lifting or, when presidents chimed in as policy partners, the arranging of final terms.[47] The point is important. It holds not just for the less activist presidents; it holds more than one might think for the Progressive-style ones. Claims that Theodore Roosevelt did this, Woodrow Wilson did this, or Franklin D.

Roosevelt (hereafter FDR) did that flow all too easily in many accounts.

The Interstate Commerce Act of 1887, the country's opening charter to regulate the railroads, came from Congress: "So far as can be determined, [Democratic President Grover Cleveland] took no part in any stage of the formulative process. In none of his messages to Congress did he mention railroad legislation. . . ."[48] Thus also the Sherman Antitrust Act of 1890, the start to an endlessly evolving policy regime affecting the structure of U.S. corporations: "[Republican] President Benjamin Harrison had taken no part in the drafting of the Sherman Act and scarcely seems to have noticed its passage."[49] Thus also the Mann-Elkins Act, railroads again, under President William Howard Taft in 1910.[50] In two instances, President Theodore Roosevelt thrust himself with consequence into ongoing congressional causes: the Hepburn Act addressing the railroads in 1905 and the Pure Food and Drugs Act of 1906, the opening regulatory move in that realm. In the latter case, a decades-long effort by a Department of Agriculture official made an impact.[51] President Woodrow Wilson certainly promoted the Federal Reserve Act of 1913, yet "the celebrated structural independence of the Fed [the Federal Reserve Board, with us still] was a product of political compromise among disparate groups represented in the U.S. Congress"—namely, "city bankers, farmers/populists, and Progressives." The design of the Fed seems to have been a resultant of those pressures rather than a carry-out of any one ex ante scheme.[52]

In later years, labor laws came from Congress. One was the still-important Davis-Bacon Act of 1931 that assures local prevailing wages on federal projects. This measure was nursed along by Republican Congresses starting in 1927, then bought into by President Herbert Hoover. A lame-duck Republican Congress passed it.[53] The Norris–La Guardia Act of 1932 curbing anti-strike injunctions and banning yellow-dog contracts was designed by academics and reformers, passed by a Democratic House and a Republican Senate, and signed by Hoover.[54] Senator Wagner's great monument, the National Labor Relations Act of 1935 or the Wagner Act, unquestionably merits the senator's name. He worked his signature design through Congress over a period of years.[55] "He was [the measure's] legislative instigator and tactician, and before Congress, the President, and the public he was its most ardent champion."[56] FDR, for his part, chimed in and championed the Wagner Act, but he was not an easy sell on it.[57]

On the taxation front, the era's first major move, although it failed, came in 1894. Congress, spurred by House member William Jennings Bryan, enacted an income tax. President Cleveland, a fellow Democrat not favoring the tax but wanting the larger measure it was attached to, let it pass absent his signature. But a conservative Supreme Court blocked it.[58] In a complicated politics in 1909, a Republican Congress roiled by a feisty Progressive faction generated the Sixteenth Amendment to the Constitution—the permanent authorization of income taxation.[59] The content of the consequent statutory income tax of 1913, backed by President Wilson, came from Congress.[60] The House result on this is said to have stemmed from interaction of three groups— leadership Democrats, radical dissenter Democrats, and Progressive Republicans.[61] The country's historic shift to a lastingly progressive revenue mix in 1916–18, including an estate tax, prompted by the military buildup needs of World War I, owed to pressure from "a powerful group of insurgent Democrats" on Capitol Hill. If you want armaments, they more or less told the (not all that reluctant) Wilson administration, we'll tax the rich to pay for them.[62] They did that.[63] Writes W. Elliot Brownlee, "The Democratic insurgents could insist that if preparedness and later the war effort were to move forward, they would do so only on the insurgents' financial terms."[64] War taxes tend to stick. Since World War I, the various rates have gone up and down, but the

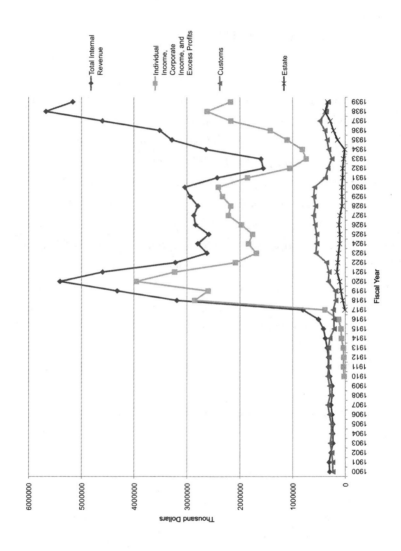

basic new *mix* created then of corporate, estate, and personal income taxes as the federal government's chief revenue reliance has stayed with us. Notably, the ruling Republicans of the later 1920s, postwar rate cutters though they were, stuck with that mix as well.[65]

That new mix and its stickiness can be seen in figure 6. The pattern shows up nicely. Yet a brief elaboration is in order. In the figure, the distance between the top line—Total Internal Revenue (that is, all revenue intake except customs duties)—and the line of progressive-leaning substance just below it—Individual Income, Corporate Income, and Excess Profits, everything in the progressive-leaning family except the low-yield estate tax—is exhausted chiefly by various excise taxes. Those are not very progressive. Boosted for World War I, the excises got another boost a decade and a half later in the Revenue Act of 1932, as can be inferred from the figure. But that desperate Depression-era measure to fill emptying coffers as people's income fell off, lowering government revenue, also brought major new affliction to the rich through its increased *rates* of personal income, corporate, and estate taxation.[66]

Those many reform decades were interesting times. In the respects noted here, Congress ordinarily took the lead. One's impression is of a

6. Sources of Federal Revenue, 1900–1939.

Sources: Prepared by John A. Dearborn. Data compiled from: Individual Income, Corporate Income, and Excess Profits and Estate Taxes: U.S. Department of the Treasury, *Annual Report of the Secretary of the Treasury on the State of the Finances for the Fiscal Year Ended June 30, 1929* (Washington, DC: U.S. Government Printing Office, 1930), pp. 419–20, table 10. U.S. Department of the Treasury, *Annual Report of the Secretary of the Treasury on the State of the Finances for Fiscal Year Ended June 30, 1939* (Washington, DC: U.S. Government Printing Office, 1940), p. 375, table 10. Total Internal Revenue and Customs: John Joseph Wallis, "Federal government revenue, by source: 1789–1939," Table Ea588–593 in Susan B. Carter et al. (eds.), *Historical Statistics of the United States, Earliest Times to the Present: Millennial Edition* (New York: Cambridge University Press, 2006), available at http://hsus.cambridge.org/ HSUSWeb/toc/tableToc.do?id=Ea588–593.

cantankerous, mercurial, free-form legislature that was often flypaper for popular impulses (although organized interests were being serviced, too). Position taking by the members to convey simple, appealing messages of blame and remedy was in style.[67] That is not distributive politics. It is populist or programmatic or ideological politics.

The Rise to World Hegemony

Following the Civil War, the United States surged in world affairs as well as in economic growth. It took a while, but it happened. It kept happening for well over a century, which makes for a long timeline in figure 1. Here I focus on U.S. projection beyond the North American continent since the 1860s. For better or worse, the United States rose to number one in world power and leadership.

In the history of this rise, what has been the place of Congress? The institution seems to have supplied a particular tilt. Not that Congress and the presidency have relentlessly disagreed on foreign policy. They have not. But often they have. Occasionally, we have seen spasms of out-front congressional action-proneness, as in the triggering of war with Spain in 1898.[68] But in general, Congress, when it has differed with the presidency on foreign policy, has leaned toward inaction, often accompanied by cacophonous talk. In a signature role, Congress has often resisted or footdragged on White House aims for expansions, invasions, intrusions, annexations, and commitments abroad. "Insularity" is a decent tagline for this bent. It entails constraint on action. Note that the idea applies to participation in multilateral agreements and commitments, not just to unilateral U.S. moves abroad.

The presidency's action-proneness is well known, but here is some of the congressional record. From the 1860s through the 1930s, presidents eyeing a takeover of colonies or dependencies often ran into

Capitol Hill resistance. Congress blocked the annexation of Santo Domingo asked by President Ulysses Grant in 1869. It delayed the absorption of the Virgin Islands and Hawaii. After the Spanish-American War of 1898, which brought the occupation of Cuba, it insisted on the Teller Amendment banning direct U.S. rule of that island. From 1900 through the 1920s, it kept putting sticks in the spokes of various presidential interventionist schemes involving Nicaragua, Haiti, and the Dominican Republic.[69] It was Congress that came to press for independence of the Philippines, annexed thanks to the Spanish-American War. In general, through an impressive variety of techniques, "Congress frequently opposed executive branch expansionist attempts through its treaty, appropriations, and investigative powers, as well as [its] informal power to shape press coverage and public opinion through public statements, nonbinding resolutions, and by simply introducing legislation."[70]

On the commitments side, Congress turned down the Versailles Treaty in 1919—which would have brought U.S. membership in the new post–World War I League of Nations—and rejected U.S. membership in the World Court in 1935.[71] In the 1930s, the Senate set the pace in American isolationism: Senator Gerald Nye's investigation blaming the munitions industry for stirring World War I brought "a daily round of headlines and sensations"—and in turn probably impaired FDR's flexibility toward aiding Britain going into 1939–41, as did a continuing Senate isolationist forcefulness right up to Pearl Harbor.[72] After World War II, all the government branches signed on to the Cold War, but foreign aid was a trial on Capitol Hill.[73] Congress, through hearings and otherwise, roused opposition to the Vietnam and Iraq wars, eventually cutting off funds in the former case and instigating the U.S. helicopter exit in 1975.[74] At several times in history, it has been leaders of the Senate Foreign Relations Committee—Charles Sumner regarding Santo

Domingo, Henry Cabot Lodge on the Versailles Treaty, William Borah on the Caribbean basin, J. William Fulbright on Vietnam—who spearheaded the opposition to White House initiatives. Three of these chairs, all but Lodge, went to the mat against presidents of their own parties.

Thus it went. And it goes on. Capitol Hill may talk, but what will it support? For presidents, the question will not go away. President Obama faced it in backing away from a military strike against Syria's Assad regime in 2013. The president decided that for legitimacy reasons he needed a congressional resolution to act, but then he apparently guessed that Congress wouldn't approve one, which it apparently wouldn't have, a turndown fate that had just struck the Tory government on the same question in the British House of Commons. So Obama backed off. In the case of Iran in 2015, he also faced the difficulty of gaining congressional support for an agreement—a multilateral commitment.

Across history, it is a story of relative congressional recessiveness. Several are the explanations given in the accounts. These have included principled anti-imperialism, inattention, costs (why not spend the war or subsidy money at home?), race in former times (why take on colonies that would dilute what once was seen as the country's white homogeneity?), lack of formal responsibility (the president is at the wheel), and, not least, institutional friction thanks to the separation-of-powers Constitution. Congress, it was once written of the Grant era, "was not blindly antiexpansionist, but it was blindly antiexecutive."[75] As a nudge to simply doing nothing, the members of Congress, for one thing, regardless of party, can be wary of taking positions that may come back and bite them later if events go wrong.[76]

The drive for Philippine independence is an interesting case. It was formally legislated (specifying a ten-year transitional lag) in the Tydings-McDuffie Act of 1934, a move to quit a colony that looks precocious against the timelines of Britain, France, and other colonial powers. This statutory drive saw a play-out of the above themes and then some on Capitol Hill. There was racism (the Filipinos were not white), principled anti-imperialism, swelling nativism and anti-immigration sentiment during the Depression, labor union alarm about wage competition against Filipinos (there was rioting in California), domestic sugar interests pressing for tariffs against Philippine products. A recent account goes: "In the Philippine case, the U.S. sugar industry was decisive in securing congressional support for decolonization. . . . [The industry] organized a pro-independence legislative coalition that paired independence for the Philippines with tariffs on Philippine exports."[77] President Hoover, conducting foreign policy and casting a strategic eye at East Asia, vetoed the version of the bill sent to him in early 1933. Soon afterward, FDR cooperated on the slightly revised final version that succeeded in 1934, but the edge for it all came from Capitol Hill.[78] (The process was complicated. Congress overrode Hoover's veto, but the Philippine colonial government bucked for a better deal, thus requiring a rewrite.)

From Jefferson's First Barbary War to Obama's use of drones, the White House has bent, at least relatively, toward international action and commitment. Congress has bent toward insularity—not always, yet recurrently. This distinction is not a surprise given the differing assignments of legislative and executive authority in the Constitution. Across history, the making of foreign policy has brought a kind of competitive channeling—the White House toward matching the British Empire or even Prussia in style and aims, Congress more comfortable with emulating something akin to a large Switzerland. It seems a good bet that this juxtaposition has contributed to a feature of American imperial reach. Of course, on this question and others, we cannot know how a non-separation-of-powers American regime would have operated during all these years, a high-in-the-sky counterfactual, but even so. The United States has accrued great influence abroad (presidents can project that), yet relatively few colonies that came to be physically possessed (Congress sometimes balked).[79] No doubt other reasons also underpin this relative lack, including basic themes of U.S. geostrategy, but presidency-Congress relations looks like one plausible cause.[80]

Foreign policy is a special realm. In international relations theory, its profile is of point-source state power that allows an exercise of instrumental rationality.[81] It is an executive profile. This policy requirement raises caution about having a strong legislature in a separation-of-powers system. In 1950, Robert A. Dahl devoted a full book to Congress's capacity, mostly its incapacity as he saw it, in foreign affairs: "Yet if one scrutinizes Congress with some care, the conclusion is unavoidable that the national legislature, as it now plays its exacting role on the political stage, is remarkably ill-suited to exercise a wise control over the nation's foreign policy."[82] This indictment came in the wake of U.S. recession from European affairs after World War I and the Congress-centered isolationism of the 1930s and 1940s.[83] If we judge institutions by their performance at times of maximum threat, Dahl's indictment is hard to get around.

Yet presidents can be troublesome, too. The appraisals of White House action and congressional opposition to it in foreign affairs have been unending and mixed.[84] Size-ups of the policies have tended to color assessments of the institutions. For the late Arthur M. Schlesinger Jr., for example, a muscle-flexing foreign-policy presidency had been a fine idea in the days of FDR and Truman, but an "imperial presidency," as he came to call it, in the days of Johnson, Nixon, and Vietnam was not. Bring back Congress.[85] In one analytic wrinkle, the good cop/bad cop presentations of the two U.S. institutions may sometimes add up to a complex exercise of instrumental rationality as other countries struggle to read the discord.[86] In effect, American head fakes have a role.

Enough said here. Yet note that to bring up instrumental rationality as the touchstone for American foreign policymaking immediately raises the question: To what end? It is a vexed topic. To pursue U.S. national welfare and security tightly defined, whatever that would be, is the obvious answer. But there have been other answers. A second is to fill the power-politics role of world hegemon. A third is to evangelize for a world order of liberal democratic capitalism. All these animations have had their influential partisans.[87]

4

Depression and the Welfare State

This chapter has an epicenter in the 1930s. I group two impulses into it—responding to the Great Depression and building a welfare state equipped with instruments of social provision. This grouping is a convenience, and it makes rough sense. As FDR and the Democrats executed their New Deal in the 1930s, they blended those two impulses. But looking back at it now, the blend was confusing and sometimes contradictory, and I take pains here to disentangle the two themes. There is also a difference in time span. Responding to the Great Depression was a 1930s drive, pure and simple. On the other topic, the Social Security Act of 1935 still enjoys its high place at the top of the American welfare state, and other significant American welfare-state moves occurred in the 1930s, hence the plausible location of the welfare state impulse in this chapter. But in fact, the timeline on building U.S. social provision runs a lot longer before and afterward. That elongation is reflected in figure 1 as well as in the discussion here.

The 1930s is ordinarily chalked up as Franklin Roosevelt's decade, and largely it was. Is the Congress of that time worth looking into at all? The answer is a clear yes. As Ira Katznelson has written, "One cannot understand the New Deal without appreciating the activist lawmaking that resulted from many bouts of arguing, bargaining, and voting in the U.S. Senate and House of Representatives. . . . In the United States, the legislature remained an effective center of political life."[1]

Responding to the Great Depression

There was no escape. Every nation had to cope with the disaster of the Great Depression that invested the world in the late 1920s. There was a universal impulse to puzzle and cope. The responses were various and have drawn immense coverage and analysis.[2] They ranged from Germany and Japan abandoning the Western trading system and liberalism in general, to the triumph of democratic socialism in Sweden, to the American New Deal.[3] Here, I emphasize the economics of the matter. What was the picture of recovery, and what explains it? There is excellent recent scholarship by economists on the U.S. policy response.

Placed in comparative perspective, how well did the U.S. policy-makers do? Generically, seems to be the answer; perhaps a bit worse than generically. They were late, for one thing. The downslide under Republican President Hoover is familiar. Then, FDR took over the presidency in 1933, and major achievement laurels still go to him as they did in the rather hagiographic scholarship of postwar years that addressed him. Yes, the recovery was slow and spotty, but, starting from a low baseline, an uptick did occur. The action was executive-led. FDR took hold as national leader in two decisive respects. On the political side, he seized control of the situation through speeches and speedy action in March 1933, thus evidently lowering the "fear," as Katznelson has written about it, that accompanied the scary and destructive banking meltdown of early 1933 during Hoover's departing lame-duck status.[4]

On the economic side, FDR quickly took the United States off the gold standard and reflated the currency. Direct White House orders were the chief instrument. These monetary moves, in what seems a surprisingly consensual view among today's economic historians, were the key to recovery. To wit: "The abandonment of the gold standard, the impact this had on the money supply, and the deliverance from the economic effects of deflation would have to be singled out as the most important contributor to the recovery." "What ends the downturn is going off gold."[5] For countries in general, the gold standard seems to have worked reasonably well before World War I, but sourly after that time and badly in the context of the Depression.[6] In addition, FDR promoted a legislative program—Congress was cooperative—that helped steady the turnaround. This brought new regulation of banking, home and farm mortgages, securities, and agricultural crop markets.[7] In the "hundred days" of legislating in the spring of 1933, "the president was always the chief orchestrator."[8] In one exception, bank deposit insurance seems to have owed chiefly to Senator Arthur Vandenberg; "It is significant that Federal Deposit insurance . . . originated in Congress."[9] In recovery terms—that is, in terms of both perking up and firming up of the economy—this variety of moves added up to a considerable success for the First New Deal of 1933–34.

Yet in the American case, the addressing of the Depression had a major additional component—*palliation,* let us call it, executed chiefly through work relief financed by the national government. That was a major thrust of the 1930s in political and provisional terms, even if it did not exactly denote or engender "recovery." Millions of jobs went on the public payroll. There, too, FDR took the lead. Work relief began in 1933 and surged in 1935 as the heavy-spending Works Progress Administration (WPA) joined the decade's list of relief agencies.[10] A good deal of money went out. "The United States became a world leader in public social spending during the Depression and did so on the basis of work and relief, not social insurance." "On the eve of the Second World War the United States pledged more of its national product to [income] security in this larger sense than any major industrial nation."[11] In a political sense, FDR and the New Deal came to be closely identified with relief spending.

Beyond these achievements, from the standpoint of either recovery or palliation, there seems less to cheer. Many of today's economic historians look back at the ambitious National Industrial Recovery Act (NIRA) of 1933, with its wage and price controls and sector-by-sector cartelizations, as a hindrance, not a help, to recovery.[12] This was a White House–led enterprise.[13] Once the Democrats and Progressives were lofted to power by the Depression, the old antimonopoly tradition flexed itself again in the 1930s. Its policy aims took on new life often as anti-depression nostrums, but it is not clear that they contributed to economic recovery. That doubt holds for the government's high-bracket tax hikes enacted in 1932 and 1935. In the 1932 case, the Hoover administration sought a tax hike to plug a major depression-induced revenue drain, and Congress's price for doing that, as in 1916, was a progressivization of the tax code.[14] The 1935 hike had FDR's stamp, as did a new tax on capital in 1936 that perhaps had an effect of dampening private investment.[15] The doubt holds for the Public Utilities Holding Company Act of 1935, for market-fettering measures like the Robinson-Patman Anti-Price Discrimination Act of 1936 and the Miller-Tydings Fair Trade Act of 1937, and for the Democrats' aggressive but apparently fruitless emphasis on antitrust action in the late 1930s.[16]

How about fiscal policy? The countercyclical thrust of U.S. government stimulus policy was relatively large in cross-national comparison,[17] spending did go out, but that thrust does not seem to have made a significant mark. Christina D. Romer writes: "[F]iscal policy, in contrast [to monetary developments], contributed almost nothing to the recovery before 1942"— that is, during World War II, which brought a huge spending stimulus.[18] A summary from several other economists goes: "Fiscal policy contributed little to the [U.S.] recovery, and certainly could have done much more."[19] At any rate, looking across a range of countries in the 1930s, austerity seems to have worked at least as well as a Keynesian countercyclical thrust.[20] In Britain, the unexciting austerity of the Tories seems to have matched, as a policy tonic perhaps bettered, the remedies of the American New Dealers.[21] Also, to rail at business firms, as John Maynard Keynes once advised FDR not to do, was not obviously a positive recovery formula.[22] In general, it is questionable to equate "the New Deal," which had its own aims and well-stocked policy content, with the era's "economic recovery achievements." One assessment goes: "The New Deal was at least as much social vision as economic recovery program. Frequently, the social vision got in the way of recovery."[23]

Congress, for its part, in the recovery actions that seem to have paid off, edged toward monetary easing in the (pre-FDR) Glass-Steagall Act of 1932—not to be confused with the identically labeled act of the next year[24]—then hastened along the relevant FDR initiatives in 1933–34, adding an ingredient of reflation in the important silver-friendly Thomas Amendment.[25] Making the currency friendly to silver was reflationary. Otherwise, the literature centering on FDR underplays the role of World War I veterans' benefits paid out in the 1930s. The veterans' interests are said to have logrolled with the silver interests in pressing their separate anti-austerity causes on Capitol Hill: "[W]hen the blocs in the two houses worked together they obtained the additional veterans' benefits and the silver legislation they were seeking."[26]

Veterans' bonuses were a very big deal in the 1930s. E. Cary Brown posted that finding decades ago,[27] and others have amplified it since. And they were entirely a congressional thrust.[28] Across the decade, insofar as U.S. countercyclical government spending did make a fiscal difference, the main factor seems to have been veterans' bonus bills enacted over presidential vetoes in 1931 (Hoover) and 1936 (FDR).[29] One sizeup of calendar 1936 goes: "Bonus payment operated as the most efficient and direct of any federal fiscal stimuli. It more quickly moved into the economy than works programs, went directly to beneficiaries, and did so without a permanent expansion of the bureaucracy. . . . The vibrancy of the 1936 economic recovery, then, can be traced almost exclusively to the Bonus payment, not the public works projects of the WPA or any other relief and recovery efforts."[30] Another: "The average bonus [of 1936] per person exceeded 30 percent of the mean household income for the veterans' age bracket. The June 1936 Federal deficit set a peacetime record of nearly one percent of the annual gross national product. In two weeks that June, veterans cashed in 46 percent of their total bonus. The economic recovery in 1936 was more than 2.5 times greater than in the preceding two years."[31] In its fiscal thrust relative to GDP, the bonus of 1936 seems to have approximated the Obama stimulus package of 2009.[32] It is hard to read these judgments without reflecting on the size of the Democratic election landslide of November 1936, which brought FDR's reelection and off-the-charts Democratic majorities on Capitol Hill. Some of the romance of the customary New Deal story goes away. That story, free with its assertions about broad voter policy judgments and consequent government policy mandates, as election stories ordinarily are, doesn't say much about the likely vote-richness of the veterans' bonuses. Generally speaking, politicians up for reelection in November will do well to send out government checks in the preceding June.

Building a Welfare State

The United States came to social provision late, has kept its public spending relatively low, and has nourished a mix of pensions and health insurance that depends uncommonly on the private sector. In these respects, this country has deviated from the European pack. There is wide agreement on these points.[33] Long-term path dependences—habits of action—extending across decades and even centuries have apparently underpinned all these tendencies. In various ways they implicate Congress.

In one interpretation, bureaucracies of a Weberian style—that is, instruments of well-ordered efficiency in Max Weber's well-known ideal type of a bureaucracy—are a precious kind of creation. In the administration of policies, they can cut down on corruption, favoritism, and fecklessness. For a society, the existence of bureaucracies like this may inspire confidence that something as complicated as a social security program might be undertaken as a government task. But the United States of the nineteenth century, a time of efficient state-building in some countries elsewhere, was relatively bureaucracy-averse. It was not very Weberian. There were various reasons for this, but one was that Congress had little appetite for building such government instruments: "The idea of imposing from above an abstract structure of positions, salaries, job qualifications, and duties on the administrative branch challenged the way Congress appropriated funds. . . . It challenged the prerogatives of congressmen to intervene in departmental affairs."[34] That lack of appetite was, among other things, a carry-through of democracy. It was a guard against elitism. On Capitol Hill, the members leaned in practice toward an ad hoc, unsightly, do-it-yourself distributive politics that did not prove a favorable advertisement for complex government action. Antiseptic administration was in short supply. The stories were damaging. Once the twentieth century rolled around, "The legacies of patronage democracy and the conjunction of its crisis in the Progressive Era created a much less favorable context for advocates of old-age pensions and social insurance" than Britain of the same time.[35]

In this regard, the United States' messy, expensive, half-century-long experience with Civil War veterans' pensions came to stand out.[36] Of the sources I consulted for this project, one real prize new to me was a long, insightful analysis of that pension system written by the prominent reformer Charles Francis Adams in 1912. This work merits a reprint and a resuscitation. Going by Adams's report of particulars, the system was trademark congressional. Its properties would fit snugly into an earlier analysis of mine, *Congress: The Electoral Connection.*[37] Policy sovereignty was located on Capitol Hill. A committee handed out particularized benefits. Individual members reveled in a credit-claiming utopia. There was state-of-the-art interest-group lobbying and a logic of program expansion. Also, there was a strong tendency toward bipartisan universalism in the enacting coalitions (at least across members of Congress from outside the South).[38] Regardless of party, the bulk of members joined in. On other evidence of this bipartisanship, nearly all the Republicans in the House plus very healthy majorities of the northern Democrats voted for final passage of the major Civil War benefits measures of 1879, 1887, 1890, 1907, and 1912 (although in 1887 the northern Democrats later successfully backed up President Cleveland's veto). Three of these measures emerged from a Democratic-controlled House. Veterans of the Union army, but not the Confederate army, could receive benefits. These specified enactments were formulaic omnibus measures. But much of the pension action was small-bore: "Congressmen intervened with the Pension Bureau to help people prove their eligibility and sponsored thousands of special pension bills tailored for individual constituents."[39] Theda Skocpol's well-known interpretation of the Civil War pension system emphasizes the parties as its venue. Certainly the parties operated as parties will do, yet in the Charles Francis Adams account, Congress comes to look like the system's basic location in analytic terms.

In light of experience like this, who, going into the twentieth century, when Germany, Britain, and Sweden led the way as welfare-state builders, would have trusted these U.S. national politicians with a huge modern pension scheme?

Recently, Monica Prasad has supplied another major interpretation of the U.S. welfare state. It has to do with the powerful antimonopolist impulse of around 1900. That impulse, which flourished in the congressional arena, not only sucked the reform oxygen into regulatory drives, it also generated a federal revenue base that even if long on tax-bracket justice was short, in ensuing generations, on money yield. Tax the rich! Yet a visible, direct, progressive system of taxation like this may be vulnerable to opposition and erosion over time and is politically hard, except in the circumstance of wars, to expand. Welfare states need money. Regressive taxes of low visibility like value-added taxes, a common European design, may supply it best.[40] On exhibit here is a path-dependent irony. American social reform earlier possibly dampened social reform later.

Since 1900, Congress and the White House have labored in the wake of these path dependences. Yet they have acted out their own distinctive proclivities. The presidency has specialized in front-page, big-bang additions to the welfare state. If possessing the White House brings out the politicians' inner Napoleon, it also brings out, to reference the mid-twentieth-century shaper of the British welfare state, their inner Clement Attlee. Thus FDR: "The Social Security Act was formulated in 1934 and guided to enactment in 1935 by Roosevelt himself and by Labor Secretary Frances Perkins. . . ."[41] FDR, in an achievement hard to classify—it entailed a kind of outsourcing of social provision—spurred the passage of the Fair Labor Standards Act of 1938, the first national minimum wage.[42] Lyndon Johnson and Congressman Wilbur Mills—the balance of influence is unclear—brought in Medicare in 1965. Barack Obama pressed for the Affordable Care Act in 2009–10. Presidents Harry Truman, Richard Nixon, and Bill Clinton aimed for comparable achievements, yet failed.[43] Perhaps Dwight Eisenhower belongs on that last list.[44] At the middle range, Clinton won his Children's Health Insurance Program (CHIP) in 1997, George W. Bush his Medicare Part D in 2003.

But Congress has been busy. In Martha Derthick's account, it "was always legislating" on social provision, even if "[i]ts normal preference was to take small steps."[45] It has initiated or joined in expansions, as of basic Social Security in 1939 and 1968–72.[46] Former congressman Henry Waxman is said to have levered a great many expansions of Medicaid: "His legislative campaigns unfold over spans of time beyond the patience of most lawmakers, and sometimes defy political gravity—in the 1980s, when anything smacking of Great Society liberalism was on the chopping block, Waxman managed to expand the Medicaid program twenty-four times."[47] To expand existent programs is a congressional trademark. Congress has also initiated new policies of the middle range—for example, the Children's Bureau in 1912, maternal benefits in 1921, disability benefits in 1956, Supplemental Security Income (SSI) in 1972, and the Earned Income

Tax Credit (EITC) in 1975. These five measures were all signed into law by Republican presidents—respectively Taft, Harding, Eisenhower, Nixon, and Ford.[48] Senator Wagner coaxed FDR into public housing subsidies in 1937.[49] GI Bills offering veterans' benefits had congressional blueprints in 1944, 1984, and 2008.[50]

Finally, much of the special private-side emphasis of American social provision owes to particular congressional initiatives that have aided the story of path dependence. Deals built into the Revenue Acts of 1942 and 1954 swerved health insurance to the private sector, where it has tended to stay. Recent historical excavation by Jacob Hacker, Christopher Howard, and Monica Prasad has brought to life these important, often overlooked ingredients of those revenue acts.[51]

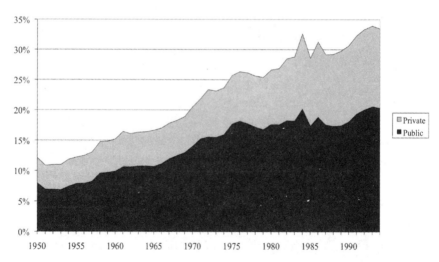

7. *Private and Public Social Welfare Expenditures as a Percentage of GDP,*
1950–1994.
Source: Figure I1.1 in Jacob S. Hacker, *The Divided Welfare State: The Battle over Public and Private Social Benefits in the United States* (New York: Cambridge University Press, 2002), 20. Originally assembled and calculated by Jacob Hacker from the Social Security Administration (SSA) social welfare expenditures series.

Member initiatives brought about private 401(k) pension plans in 1978 and the Employee Retirement Income Security Act (ERISA) supplying guarantees for private pensions in 1974.[52] Assisting this private-side emphasis, according to an interpretation by Kimberly J. Morgan and Andrea Louise Campbell, is a chronic need to forge enactment deals that assemble broad, interest-diverse coalitions so as to master Capitol Hill veto points.[53]

All told, the American welfare state is a vastly intricate system that keeps evolving substantially at congressional behest showing a congressional spin. A nutshell presentation of that evolution from 1950 through the mid-1990s, showing the shares between public and private-side provision, can be seen in figure 7.

5

After World War II

In this chapter I enter times that some of us can remember. I take up three impulses of the post–World II era, allowing that era to sprawl into the 1980s. These impulses are not tightly related to each other. Two of them deal with the economy, bracketing its course from an inspiration flowing out of the war through an ideological and policy retake a generation later. The other impulse covers one of the major developments of American, not to mention transnational, history— the civil rights revolution of those times. Economic planning devices, energy supply, the cities, travel, infrastructure, the tax code, industrial structure, the workplace, immigration, demographic patterns, the electorate, rights standards, relations among the races, and much else gained lasting imprints from U.S. government participation in the three impulses discussed here.

Postwar Prosperity

A spirit of "never again," looking back at the privations of the Depression years, seems to have invested American politics as World War II came to a close. In short order, the mission to conduct the Cold War added another reason to make the economy hum. Armaments needed to be funded, allies to be braced up, the Soviet Union to be kept ahead of. In the realm of ideas, American leaders "came to emphasize economic productivity as a principle of political settlement in its own right."[1] Growth, development, efficiency, and productivity took on value as a family of policy aims. Eisenhower and Kennedy, the presidents from 1953 through 1963, are said to have specialized in "economic ideologies" that hinged on long-term economic soundness and growth.[2]

In the United States and elsewhere, prosperity and growth did indeed soar for a quarter-century or so. This country set the pace. "From 1950 through 1970, by fits and starts, the American Gross National Product grew at an average annual rate of 3.9 percent, perhaps the best performance in the nation's history."[3] Yet postwar Europe joined the spirit and practices: "Economic growth became a universal creed and a common expectation to which governments were expected to conform."[4] With consequence: "Less than a decade after staggering uncertainly out of the rubble, Europeans entered, to their amazement and with some consternation, upon the age of affluence."[5] In hindsight, for the developed world, these "golden years" have come to seem like "an altogether exceptional phase of history; perhaps a unique one."[6] Figure 8, although ragged, exhibits the height of the U.S. growth rate during the decades after 1950 or so and the decline since that time.

Generally speaking, the American program for postwar prosperity was executive-led. It is a complicated story. The era's liberals aimed for a huge dose of top-down planning of the economy, but they missed. Congress would not go along. The National Resources Planning Board, a nursery of liberal ideas, had its funding ended by a conservative-leaning Congress in 1943. The Employment Act of 1946, even if a historic move, lost much of its aimed-for planning authority on the way to enactment.[7] Still, the executive branch flourished. Harry Dexter White of the Treasury Department led the authoring of the World

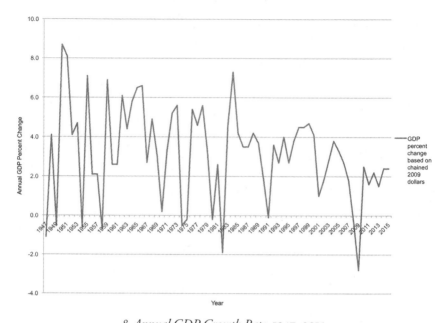

8. Annual GDP Growth Rate, 1947–2015.
Source: Prepared by John A. Dearborn. U.S. Department of Commerce, Bureau of Economic
Analysis, available at www.bea.gov/national/index.htm#gdp.

Bank and the International Monetary Fund at the Bretton Woods
conference in 1944. A largely clueless Congress signed on.[8] Bolstered
by the war experience, a new executive enterprise—Keynesian, exper-
tise-based agenda-setting for the economy so as to allow adjustment
of employment, growth, and price levels—came into its own and
proved long-lasting and (evidently) successful. The government's war
experience had "institutionalized structural Keynesianism."[9] The
Employment Act of 1946, edited to congressional size though it was,
creating the Council of Economic Advisers, gave this Keynesian
regime authorization and shape.[10] It was a presidency-centered regime.

Otherwise, the postwar presidents had their particular policy em-
phases. Eisenhower, for one thing, was a promoter and builder. It is

something of a surprise, given his customary laid-back image. There is wonderful bragging material in his memoirs. The country's power electric facilities, he wrote, were built "on a scale historically unprecedented" during his presidency. In January 1953, there was "a total installed capacity of 97.3 million kilowatts. By January of 1960 that figure had soared to 175 million—almost twice as much."[11] This reads like a bulletin from the Kremlin in the 1930s. The new interstate highway system of the 1950s was "the biggest peacetime construction project of any description ever undertaken by the United States or any other country." Building it would "move enough dirt and rock to bury all of Connecticut two feet deep."[12] The Upper Colorado River Storage Project, with its big dams and creation of Lake Powell, was "the largest reclamation project ever authorized in a single piece of legislation."[13]

Kennedy, in the economic sphere, stands out for his drives to free up international trade and to cut taxes so as to promote long-term economic growth—not just to nudge short-term stimulation of the economy. In the Kennedy tax cut of 1964 (enacted posthumously), the top-bracket income tax rate came down permanently from 91 percent to 70 percent.[14]

On exhibit here, however, is the role of Congress. Beyond the new Keynesian management, an executive-level task once it was authorized, the country's postwar drive toward growth, development, productivity, and the rest, from Truman's presidency through Kennedy's, was very much a legislative thrust—a record of lawmaking, one act after another. All the Eisenhower and Kennedy items mentioned above exemplify that. It was a big legislative era. It is not often seen as one. It ran short on polarizing pyrotechnics and showdowns. Also, its policy achievements lacked the "progressive" profile that is often taken as a necessary indicator that any policy action is going on at all. "Not much happened" is a conventional assessment of this postwar era from the standpoint of progressive or liberal reform agendas. That is the tenor of, for example, James L. Sundquist's memorable account of legislating in *Politics and Policy: The Eisenhower, Kennedy, and Johnson Years*.[15] But that is a partisan account. Of the era's actual key enactments, senators of a leftist persuasion went to the wall filibustering against three of them—atomic energy and oil drilling measures backed by Eisenhower and the launch of a communications satellite corporation (a joint public/private affair) backed by Kennedy. "Give-aways" of the public domain, these measures were seen as. But they passed.[16]

In the era's legislating, cooperation between presidents and cross-party congressional majorities was a common pattern. I am interested here in enactments aimed at some mix of economic growth, development, efficiency, and productivity. See table 2 for a selected list. It runs from late Truman (1949–52) through Eisenhower (1953–60) and Kennedy (1961–63). The thrusts of the two Truman-era items pinpointed here, urban renewal and peer review in science research, were not New Deal–ish or Fair Deal–ish in spirit. Those two innovative flourishes came from Congress. Ushered into existence by statute during the full era were urban renewal, support of science research, offshore oil drilling, a private atomic energy industry, "flexible prices" in agriculture, the Saint Lawrence Seaway allowing ocean ships to reach Minnesota, the forty-two-thousand-mile interstate highway system, the Upper Colorado project (big dams) channeling water use for the Southwest, support of science education, the space program, area redevelopment, and the communications satellite.[17] Reduction of international trade barriers proceeded under Eisenhower in 1955 and Kennedy in 1962.

Interestingly, many of the moves of Eisenhower's first term were in policy areas that had gotten stalemated as the twenty years of Democratic control of the government under FDR and Truman ran on to

Table 2. Enactments Promoting Growth, Development, Efficiency, or Productivity under Truman (second term), Eisenhower, and Kennedy

Provision	Year	Statute that included the provision
Urban renewal	1949	Housing Act
	1954	Housing Act
Peer review in science research	1950	National Science Foundation Act (NSF)
Offshore oil drilling	1953	Submerged Lands Act (regarding "tidelands")
	1953	Outer Continental Shelf Lands Act
Saint Lawrence Seaway	1954	Saint Lawrence Seaway Act
Private atomic energy industry	1954	Atomic Energy Act
Flexible crop prices	1954	Agricultural Act
Growth-friendly taxes	1954	Internal Revenue Act
	1962	Revenue Act (investment tax credit)
	1964	Revenue Act (the "Kennedy tax cut," posthumous)
Freed-up foreign trade	1955	Reciprocal Trade Agreements Act extension
	1958	Reciprocal Trade Agreements Act extension
	1962	Trade Expansion Act
Colorado River project	1956	Colorado River Storage Project Act
Interstate highway system	1956	Federal-Aid Highway Act
Space program	1958	National Aeronautics and Space Act (NASA)
Science education	1958	National Defense Education Act (NDEA)
Area redevelopment	1961	Area Redevelopment Act
Communications satellite	1962	Communications Satellite Act (COMSAT)

a dispiriting close during the Korean War. Conflict about them had carried on, but nothing was happening. Action stirred under full Republican control of the government in 1953–54 or during divided party control after the 1954 midterm. That point holds, for example, for offshore drilling (a new technological frontier), crop subsidies (why keep funding expensive overproduction?), atomic energy (how to develop it?), the seaway (why not build it?), and the interstate highway system (same question).

Certainly, many of these policy moves have drawn mixed reviews since. We read about air pollution, dreary strip malls, gooey oil spills, nuclear-plant troubles at Three Mile Island, oceanic zebra mussels invading the Great Lakes, freeway murderers on the new interstates, and so on.[18] But they were substantial, consequential moves. The late Daniel Patrick Moynihan, an urban scholar among other roles, sized up the new highway system thus in 1970: "This was a program which the twenty-first century will almost certainly judge to have had more influence on the shape and development of American cities, the distribution of population within metropolitan areas and across the nation as a whole, the location of industry and various kinds of employment opportunities (and, through all these, immense influence on race relations and the welfare of black Americans) than any initiative of the middle third of the twentieth century." It was, wrote Moynihan in the spirit of Eisenhower, the largest public works program in history.[19] The map in figure 9 shows its eventual nationwide scope highway-by-highway with the routes numbered.

In terms of economic growth, the impact of these various policy moves is hard to gauge, although especially the "infrastructure investment" of the highway program, to use an organizing buzz-term from the economics journals, has drawn interest.[20] Regarding the new highways, "It is worth noting," Robert J. Shiller comments, "that the U.S. achieved its fastest economic growth since 1929 in the 1950s and 1960s, a time of high government expenditure on the Interstate Highway System, which was launched in 1956."[21] U.S. infrastructure spending has tailed off since the 1960s.[22]

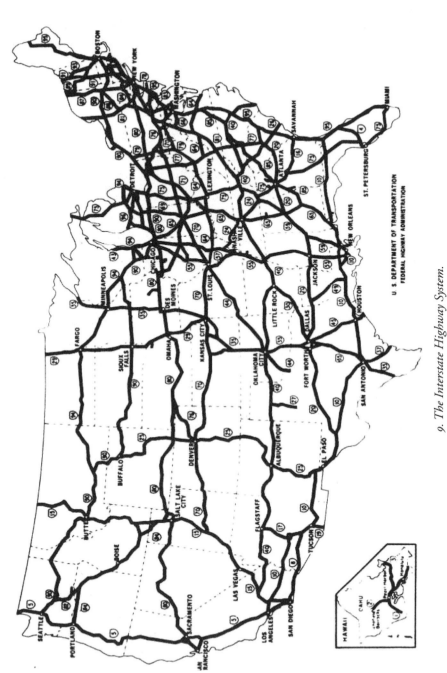

9. *The Interstate Highway System.*

Source: U.S. Department of Transportation, Federal Highway Administration, available at www.fhwa.dot.gov/interstate/finalmap.cfm.

At any rate, we see here an era of surprisingly active lawmaking of a particular content and coalitional style. It has not drawn a great deal of notice as such.

Civil Rights

The American South had a slave system, then, after an interlude during Reconstruction after the Civil War, a racial caste system. Through the 1930s, that caste system stayed deeply embedded. Jim Crow separatism is said to have "reached its perfection in the 1930s," by which time it "prevailed throughout the South in all aspects of life, everywhere one looked."[23] Revealingly, at the level of electoral positioning and lawmaking, no twentieth-century American president took a serious interest in civil rights before World War II. That holds for FDR in the 1930s.

Then came the consciousness-raising shock of World War II and the ensuing civil rights revolution. In an American war drive that came to target racism (at least in the European theater) and that required mobilization of the full home population, how could this country's racist traditions be accommodated any longer?[24] President Harry Truman was quick off with public support of civil rights in 1946.[25] One indicator of the swift, substantial change in public views is the diverging reception accorded to Democratic Senator Theodore G. Bilbo of Mississippi, perhaps the century's most flagrant congressional racist. In the late 1930s Bilbo rattled on in astonishingly vicious public statements. It was the way of the Senate. Why even take notice? But by 1947, if Bilbo had not been near death at that time, the newly Republican-run Senate was apparently fixing to bar him from his seat for the same kinds of statements.[26] In an immediate, little-known backwash of the war, the territory of Alaska seems to have set a precedent in abolishing its Jim Crow laws in 1945. (Alaska's native population, still large today, was proportionately larger then.)[27] Soon, the waging of U.S. foreign policy in the context of the Cold War added another major spur to the civil rights cause.

But the postwar civil rights drive took place elsewhere, too, not just in the United States. One comparison goes: "Like many successful revolutions, the [American] civil rights revolution was disguised as a restoration [a reference to post–Civil War Reconstruction in the 1860s]. But in reality it was part of a global process of overturning white supremacy and white colonialism that occurred simultaneously throughout the world in the decades following World War II. The other English-speaking democracies—Britain, Canada, Australia, and New Zealand—all abolished their white-supremacist civil rights laws and white-only immigration policies at the same time that the United States did. . . ."[28] The analogy to the British settler colonies with their indigenous racial minorities seems especially apt. It is not exact: The United States alone among them had a large ex-slave African American population. But in all those countries, as in the United States, we see a buildup of public sentiment and civil-rights movement activity ending in policy changes in the 1960s and 1970s. Societal pressure, cresting in leadership by the Reverend Martin Luther King Jr. in the 1960s, seems to have been especially prominent in the United States.

The United States guaranteed its voting rights across racial lines in 1965, Canada in 1960, Australia in 1967.[29] The United States passed its anchoring Civil Rights Act—the Public Accommodations Act—in 1964. Canada issued a white paper in 1969 proposing complete formal rights for the country's Indians (who, however, for anti-assimilationist reasons, rejected the idea). Australia brought a range of civil rights to its Aborigines between the late 1950s and mid-1970s.[30] Violent confrontations offered a counterpoint to these advances: One source likens America's Little Rock confrontation in 1957—could the Arkansas schools be desegregated in the face of violence?—to London's Notting Hill clash in 1958 and South Africa's Sharpeville clash in 1960.[31] South Africa was another British (and Dutch) settler colony, although unlike the others it was chiefly nonwhite.

Otherwise, facing the outside world, the United States deracialized its immigration policy in 1965: This country's Europe-friendly "national origins quotas" were abandoned. Australia moved that way in the mid-1960s, New Zealand in 1974.[32] Canada backed away from its Eurocentric immigration in 1962.[33] At the level of party positioning, the Australian Labor Party, matching America's Democratic Party in a nice analogy, completed a historic U-turn from being a stern guardian of white privilege to being a special champion of universal rights.[34] For the Australian party, the chief target had been Asian immigration, although the American Democrats had been anti-Asian, too (as well as anti-black); consider the American party's out-front nineteenth-century campaign for Chinese exclusion or President Woodrow Wilson's anti-Japanese stance at the Paris peace conference after World War I.[35] A deft study comparing the turnarounds by these left-of-center Australian and American parties is in order; I have not come across one. All told, across the various countries, there was a good deal of parallel evolution after World War II. South Africa reformed later, but the Sharpeville massacre that triggered a long mobilization in that country occurred in 1960. A pro-rights zeitgeist seems to have been at work. During this same era, colonies with black populations in central Africa and the West Indies were gaining independence.[36] On the example of the 1960s, to carry the case farther than I will go here, rights claims for groups beyond race came to proliferate in the United States and societies elsewhere.

If the United States addressed civil rights on a common transnational calendar, there was of course variety across its institutions. The

courts and the executive branch led the American civil rights revolution. That is abundantly clear.[37] The Supreme Court's decisions are
well known. Presidents Truman, Eisenhower, Kennedy, and Johnson
pressed in turn for legislation.

Congress lagged behind in a familiar historical pattern. The
Senate's well-known filibuster process, which can register differences
in intensity among the members, allowed holdups of legislative
action. Senators from the intensely anti–civil rights white South,
where the bulk of African Americans could not vote, faced off against
senators from the generally pro–civil rights but lukewarm North.
That was the chronic story from 1890 into the 1960s.[38] Again and
again, bills passed by the House—the chief topics were anti-lynching
and voting rights—died in the Senate. That happened in 1890–91,
1922, 1938, 1940, 1942, 1944, 1946, 1948, 1949–50, and 1956. Other
bills, as in 1957 and 1960, were watered down in the Senate.[39]

In general terms, it is easy to view the history of the Senate filibuster indiscriminately across all kinds of issues as a display of antiseptic
statistics—numbers of cloture votes (that is, moves to cut off debate),
numbers of bills blocked, hours spent in windy speeches of this or
that length, and so on. Yet really, in this institutional hold-up practice, race relations was not just another issue. Race was *at the center
of* the development and maintenance of the Senate's supermajority
customs during the long middle stretch of the South's racial caste system. To protect their sectional interests, the southerners seem to have
nursed along anti–majority-rule supermajoritarianism as a general
way of conducting the chamber's business. Shrewdly, they saw that
"broad majorities of the Senate might vote for civil rights measures
if given the chance, meaning that Southerners might lose more
than they gain if the Senate began applying cloture against all filibusters. Over time, some Southerners began to view cloture voting as a

logroll—if I don't vote to end your filibuster [on whatever issue] even though I disagree with you, you don't vote for cloture against me."[40] That was the background as the Senate accommodated the country's great intensity chasm on race during the several generations. Then, the pattern broke in the 1960s as the regional intensities more or less equilibrated in public opinion and on Capitol Hill. In the North, pro–civil rights sentiment grew stronger. In the white South, backing of the traditional caste system, for all the region's resistance in the 1960s, faltered. At that point, the Senate's civil rights filibusters could be bypassed or broken. The major statutes—the Civil Rights Act of 1964 and the Voting Rights Act of 1965—hence passed and they could also be enforced.[41] Often, passing laws is not enough. Enforcement of the Reconstruction era's laws had been a huge, often perilous difficulty in earlier times.

Affirmative action—that is, racial preferences as a service to dis-criminated-against minorities—is a later and somewhat different story. On this front, the executive branch unquestionably took the lead. Federal officials moved to affirmative action in the late 1960s and 1970s through an apparent mix of policy belief, leeway inhering in the bureaucracy, White House leadership (by Presidents Johnson and Nixon), interest group networking by civil rights advocates, and a concern for public order.[42] Executive leaders worry about public order, as they had done in the southern confrontations over civil rights in Arkansas, Mississippi, and Alabama in the 1950s and early 1960s. The ensuing years also brought race-related disorder, this time in the cities of especially the North.[43] Bureaucrats went at the new policy inventiveness beaverishly: In one account, "The race-conscious model of hard affirmative action was developed in trial-and-error fashion by a coalition of mostly white, second-tier civil servants in the social service agencies of the presidency."[44] Congress proved wary of affirmative action but swerved into support for minority contract set-asides in 1977 that specified six racial minorities. In one interpretation, this was "a tour de force of policy entrepreneurship by leaders of the civil rights coalition in Congress."[45] Here we see a coalitional strategy that can be executed in legislatures and is familiar from the days of the traditional tariff. Claimants with similar aspirations can join in a principle and pool their intensities in a relation of "reciprocal noninterference."

Neoliberalizing the Economy

The 1970s brought challenge to the world's economies. Command systems in the Communist East, corporatism in Europe, and Keynesianism in the Anglophone world came under pressure as their various hierarchical techniques seemed to falter.[46] Stagflation, inflation, low growth, and other economic stucknesses were being met with intellectual paralysis. Ready with a body of ideas accenting microeconomics and market efficiencies, academic economists fostered a shift to neoliberal remedies. (Let there be no confusion here: *Neoliberal* refers to *liberalism* in its traditional European sense of free-market friendliness, not to the way Americans use the term *liberal* today in ordinary discourse.)

At this juncture, ideational change seems to have led the way to policy change.[47] That can be one causal path to change, and apparently, at least in large part, here was an instance. One account offers a historical parallel: "[T]he shift in public opinion in the 1970s, like the shift in the 1930s, was preceded by a shift among economists." Back then, the journals had been filling up with explanations and prescriptions inviting to the New Deal's enterprises; now, neoliberal ideas had become the rage.[48] At any rate, deregulation, privatization, lower taxes, weaker labor unions, and a reshuffle of causal stories regarding the economy surged in the 1970s and 1980s as public agenda content. "Welfare" inched into "workfare" as an ethos of the welfare state.[49] Market-friendly locutions surged in media use.[50]

The United States joined other countries in these developments— probably a bit ahead. Neoliberalism set in all over the place: One account tells of the varying routes to it in Chile, Britain, Mexico, and France.[51] Yet especially plain is the commonality of policy movement across the Anglophone countries—Britain, Canada, Australia, New Zealand, and the United States.[52] In New Zealand, it was the Labor Party that carried some especially vigorous neoliberal reforms. Academics fresh from U.S. graduate economics programs, it is said, infused neoliberal ideas into a powerful New Zealand government bureaucracy waved on by a party leader hankering for innovation.[53] It was the way to go.

Keynesianism went out, alternative ideas came in. Ronald Reagan targeted taxes, labor unions, and regulations.[54] Simultaneously in the 1980s, Margaret Thatcher in Britain targeted unions and pressed for privatization of housing stock and industries. Yet in this country a good deal of the policy evolution took place earlier in the 1970s in advance of the 1980 election and Reagan's presidency. President Jimmy Carter, not Reagan, appointed Paul Volcker to the Federal Reserve, where Volcker broke orthodoxy to advance new anti-stagnation policies. Reagan as president then backed him up.[55] The drive to deregulate industries began in the 1970s, and "within a very short time" it was "transformed from a lonely cause with poor political prospects into a buzzword and bandwagon."[56] In Senate hearings on airline deregulation in 1975: "Witnesses from the airlines and from the CAB [Civil Aeronautics Board] found it impossible to rebut the critical [pro-deregulation] logic of Senator [Edward] Kennedy and his well-prepared staff." As in New Zealand, here was deregulation from the left.[57] A 1978 enactment undid the airlines' old "iron triangle" of interests. Deregulation of the railroads, also completed under Carter, was "swift and staggering." In that case, "A widely disparaged idea, launched by a rather inexperienced staff working for an unpopular administration and receiving only lukewarm assistance from the industry's leaders, was changing the century-old way railway economics worked."[58] Otherwise, constraints were loosened in those years on trucking, banking, and telecommunications.[59] Price controls on oil and natural gas were phased out in 1978–81.[60]

As for the government branches, both the presidency and Congress pressed for tax cuts in the years around 1980. Preceding the well-known Reagan cuts of 1981 was the Revenue Act of 1978—"a major milestone in federal tax policy," enacted by a Democratic Congress—which slashed capital gains taxes. This measure "dramatically reversed the reform orientation of the 1969 and 1976 revenue acts and thereby laid the groundwork for the even more sweeping changes in federal tax policy that took place in 1981."[61] The slash took place on Capitol Hill, but it was not just a congressional move: Quickly evolving ideas within the executive branch are said to have contributed to it.[62] The Kemp-Roth plan, a blueprint for the across-the-board tax cuts of 1981, was hatched and merchandised by members of Congress.[63] Reducing taxes around this time seems to have had popular roots, as in California's slash of property taxes through Proposition 13. It was not just an ideological or partisan platform.[64]

On the deregulation side, the Gerald Ford and Carter administrations ordinarily took the lead in the 1970s.[65] In the airlines case, the executive branch's CAB leadership swung into advocacy for deregulation. But Congress was a major player, too—notably in pressing to decontrol energy prices. On the airlines, the main opposition to deregulation came from the industry's companies and unions.[66] Aside from widespread complaints about lines at the gas pumps, probably no one would claim that the deregulative activity of this era had much in the way of popular roots. Often, as in energy politics, it had some industry impetus. Yet it seems to have issued chiefly from the academics, the bureaucrats, and the elected officials.

The neoliberal impulse was a surprising and powerful thing. Of course, there were partisan differences. Reagan and Thatcher had their slants. For one thing, no left-of-center party would have gone after the unions the way they did, and the two leaders shared an ideological force and purism. Yet, looked at in cold historical perspective, the neoliberal impulse was all-around pervasive in the United States. Even if not in all its particulars, it infused both the presidency and Congress, the Republican and Democratic parties, the presidential administrations of the two parties, and the politics of two adjoining decades.

6

The Climate and the Debt

In this work, I steer clear of various impulses, causes, or angsts that inhabit the headlines of today but that are hard to get a historical bead on yet. We do not know where these concerns are going. There is jihadi terrorism. There is spiraling immigration into the rich Western countries. There is growing inequality in income and wealth. There is unease about globalization. All are concerns of transnational incidence, but I am leaving them and others alone. In the case of the growing inequality, for example, we do not know whether the idea of tackling it somehow can come to enjoy serious traction, beyond a sector of intellectuals and activists, as a political cause. A century ago, in the remarkably forceful tax-the-rich campaign waged by U.S. Progressive reformers in a somewhat similar context, the answer was yes. But today, so far anyway, the response in the United States and elsewhere has been sluggish. A great many concerns, we should be aware, keep simmering at a low level or just go away. They do not spur chapters in the history books.

But two major impulses of transnational incidence do have action blotters extending back decades, even if they carry on today. They are unfinished impulses, so to speak. They present themselves to us as challenges still on the table. Yet they have a record.

Climate Change

There are occasions when politics meets science. This is one of them. But there is a twist. Once, the United States set the world pace in regulating the environment. That was a time before "climate change" or "global warming" emerged as a specific concern. But regarding environmental regulation in general, a U.S. policymaking lineage extends backward, and, especially with Congress in mind, it makes sense to begin a discussion with that earlier experience.

Here is that early experience, as summarized by David Vogel: "From the 1960s through the mid 1980s American regulatory standards [on consumer as well as environmental questions] tended to be more stringent, comprehensive and innovative than in either individual European countries or in the European Union (EU)."[1] Clean air, clean water, auto emissions, oil spills, endangered species, pesticides, toxic substances, hazardous waste, forest management—name a topic and Congress was there bearing a law. See table 3 for a selected list of such statutes enacted from the mid-1960s through the mid-1970s.

Generally speaking, this was a congressional realm. The presidents tended toward being passive or reactive. The Johnson administration did weigh in, but its major policy concerns lay elsewhere in those times. Democratic senator Edmund Muskie often took an environmental lead during Johnson's years and later. Sometimes President Nixon is credited with environmental reform. He assembled the Environmental Protection Agency (EPA) by executive order, a major move. On the legislative side, there are "Nixon did this" stories. But those stories have limited grounding. Once, in a search for Nixon's legislative agenda that the White House actually spent much attention and energy on, I came up with little about the environment.[2] For the most part, Nixon signed bills sent up by Democratic Congresses, sometimes

Table 3. Environmental Regulation Statutes Enacted During 1963–1976

Year	Statute
During Johnson Presidency:	
1963	Clean Air Act
1964	Wilderness Act
1965	Highway Beautification Act (ban on billboards)
1965	Motor Vehicle Air Pollution Control Act
1965	Water Quality Act
1965	Solid Waste Disposal Act
1966	Clean Air Act amendments (aid to states and local communities)
1968	National Trails System Act
During Nixon and Ford Presidencies:	
1969	National Environmental Policy Act (NEPA, source of environmental impact statements)
1970	Clean Air Act – the big one
1970	Water Quality Improvement Act (aimed at oil spills, sewage)
1972	Water Pollution Control Act (the main one)
1972	Marine Mammal Protection Act
1972	Ocean Dumping Act
1972	Pesticide Control Act
1972	Coastal Zone Management Act
1973	Endangered Species Act
1974	Safe Drinking Water Act
1976	Toxic Substances Control Act
1976	National Forest Management Act
1976	Federal Land Policy and Management Act
1976	Resource Conservation and Recovery Act (regulation of hazardous wastes)

claiming credit for them. Congress enacted one of the major instruments, the Water Quality Control Act of 1972, over a Nixon veto.[3]

On Capitol Hill, this was a classic position-taking politics. Even if the measures themselves were often complex, indeed sometimes thick and elaborate beyond belief, tales of blame and remedy were simple and conveyable. Being on the side of reform looked good. Often the reformer Ralph Nader, with his extraordinary capacity to stir public awareness and alarm, was at the back of the drives. In the face of opposition that was weak, nonexistent, or capable of adapting easily enough to reform, much could be legislated and was. Clearly, in the long frame of things, there is nothing inherent in the processes of Congress that wards off regulating the environment.

In recent decades, however, as the environmental cause has morphed into "global warming" and "climate change," Europe has surged forward and the United States has become, also according to David Vogel in a 2003 assessment, a "regulatory laggard."[4] A 2005 study rich in statistical comparisons across a range of regulatory areas found that "Europe became relatively more precautionary [that is, more regulatory than the United States] during the 1990s and the early 2000s." This finding was notably true for "ecological risk."[5]

On the legislative front, few new American laws have emerged. Famously in 1997, during the Clinton presidency, the Senate gave a preemptive thumbs-down to the Kyoto Protocol, the high-profile multi-nation treaty of that year setting limits on greenhouse gas emissions. That is, the Senate signaled no even before the plan was internationally agreed to—by a vote of 95–0. No support for it at all. Why did Clinton go on to sign the protocol facing such Senate headwinds for ratification? No doubt the motivation was mixed, yet in a recent academic study based on interviews with expert Kyoto participants from Norway, Germany, and the United States, the leading explanation is an exercise of noninstrumental—or at least noninstrumental in immediate formal terms—position taking by the Clinton White House.[6] Under Obama, a cap-and-trade bill passed the Democratic House in 2009, but the process for that was tortuous and stirred opposition, and the bill went nowhere in the Democratic Senate.

Why this new reluctance?[7] Certainly, in the United States or anywhere, today's "climate change" drive is hitting understandable difficulties. These include collective-action misfirings among nation-states, a causal path to future doom that is cloudy and stubbornly disputed,[8] and cognitive deficiencies that may hobble us all in assessing risk.[9] American public opinion, compared with that abroad, has been relatively lax. In a study reported in 2012, the United States ranked forty-first out of forty-seven countries in "concern for global warming."[10] American media interest can be sluggish.[11] We may be seeing a case of alarm fatigue abetted by a shortage of disasters that are credibly connectable to climate change (although not for a lack of nominations). There is a recent lack of "focusing events."[12] Scattered stories about hurricanes or polar bears are not enough.

But of particular interest here are institutional factors. Recent presidents, at least the Democratic ones, have pressed, sometimes crusaded, for climate change action. Executive directives have abounded. But Congress has been more passive or hostile. Probably one reason is that environmental reform has shifted toward being a quest for international commitments—ordinarily a hard sell on Capitol Hill. Politically speaking, the Senate's thumbs-down to the Kyoto Protocol seems like a cousin to, say, its thumbs-down to the World Court in the 1930s. In cases like these, Congress has shied away from U.S. enlistment in binding international rules. Also, environmental politics in its global phase has come to map onto partisan polarization as it had not done in the 1960s and 1970s, with the Republican Party increasingly frosty to both diagnoses and remedies. Here we see a venerable theme. The Republicans in Congress and elsewhere, going back a century and a half, have had a special favor for American nationalism. This is an unfavorable prompt for internationalism.[13]

All this having been said, on current evidence it is not clear that peer countries are actually digging their teeth much deeper into climate change than the Americans. Poor economic times have been threatening the affordability of Europe's ambitious formal commitments.[14] There are scorecard studies. In a 2014 Organization for Economic Cooperation and Development (OECD) report on "environmental policy stringency" across twenty-four OECD countries, the United States ranked fifteenth in climate-control progress—behind, for example, the Scandinavian countries, the Netherlands, Germany, Canada, and Japan but ahead of, for example, Britain, France, Australia, Italy, and Belgium.[15] In these rankings, there is not much to be said for a distinctive American exceptionalism spoking off in any direction.

Long-Run Debt and Deficit

There are occasions when politics meets arithmetic. Since the early 1970s, the developed countries have suffered a slowed economic growth yet kept running up expenditures, thus putting pressure on debt/deficit—let us say on long-run fiscal balance. The free-spending mindset of the booming economies of the 1950s and 1960s has been hard to shed. Generally speaking, government outlays and commitments to future outlays have kept rising. Revenues have not risen so much.

In a nutshell, here is the U.S. performance in comparative perspective: In long-term trends, sorry though they may be, this country has performed as one of the pack. In the last decade or so, to consider that span in particular, American remedial action regarding debt/deficit has apparently stood up well in comparison. On the various numbers, there does not seem to be a case for the United States as a serious upside or downside outlier.[16] As of 2011, the United States ranked thirteenth in public debt as a percentage of GDP in a comparison set of thirty-one peer countries (number one means highest debt). Freer of debt were, for example, Spain, the Netherlands, Poland, Switzerland, and Australia. Deeper in debt were, for example, all the other allied OECD G8 countries—that is, all the other big Western-type economies—Japan, Italy, France, Canada, Germany, and Britain.[17] Given the trends, of course, this American near-averageness does not point to a carefree future.[18]

How about the U.S. institutions? Does this country's worsening fiscal plight, or its lackadaisical remediation of that plight, owe in distinctive traces to the structure or practices of its institutions—Congress and the rest? Can we see any smoking guns? There is a line-up of usual suspects. At the most general level, does having a mixed presidency–cum–legislature system all by itself, as opposed to the streamlinedness of parliamentary government, cause fiscal problems? Apparently not. If anything, the relation may go the other way. According to one cross-national assessment, "Presidential systems matter for budget balances because they generate relatively high incentives for governments to keep budgets under control."[19]

How about divided party control of the government—that is, when the presidency, the House, and the Senate are not simultaneously controlled by one party? We have had a good deal of that dividedness—more than 60 percent of the time since World War II. I do not see a credible case that fiscal management has fared worse under conditions of divided control. Fortunately, in an analytic sense, there is experience to compare. Necessarily, the history offers only small data for recent times, but take some telling instances. Deficits accumulated under Reagan (divided control), but they also drew force under George W. Bush in 2001 and 2003–06 and under Obama in 2009–10 (all unified). Taming of deficits occurred under Clinton in

1993–94 (unified) but also under George H. W. Bush in 1989–90 and Clinton in 1995–2000 (divided).[20] In the case of Obama and the Democrats in 2009–10, there is the obvious point that it made sense to run a deficit to soften the Wall Street crash.

Yet the full record of Obama's first term shows the limits of a divided-versus-unified logic as well as something else—the surprising flexibility of the U.S. system. For one thing, the United States placed very high in the size (relative to GDP) of its countercyclical fiscal package in 2008 and calendar 2009, the recent crash juncture. It ranked first among thirty-three countries in one study,[21] third among twenty-three in another (only Iceland and Spain ran ahead).[22] This was a crisis-time win for Keynesian macroeconomics. The Obama stimulus to the economy was big. Yet during the ensuing Congress of 2011–12, a time of divided party control after the Republicans swept the House in the 2010 midterms, the government subtracted a projected $2.7 trillion from the debt/deficit. That is, it subtracted $900 billion directly plus another $1.2 trillion through a delayed "sequestration" in the Budget Control Act of August 2011, then another $600 billion through the chiefly high-bracket tax hikes pressed for by Obama in the "fiscal cliff" deal following his 2012 reelection.[23] Notably, the dollar effects of sequestration stuck in place for quite a while after passage. In the cases of both the sequestration and the fiscal cliff, the policy achievements at the times of passage were obscured by the ugly optics of the enactment processes. Who will forget the standoffs between President Obama and House Speaker John Boehner, the government-shutdown script, and all the rest? But the $2.7 trillion subtraction was huge. It seems to have dwarfed the much-dwelt-on earlier fiscal settlements achieved in 1990 and 1993 under respectively George H. W. Bush and Clinton. As of early 2015, thanks partly to an improving economy yet still traveling under divided party control of the government, the U.S. federal budget deficit (as a share of GDP) had fallen below a forty-year average.[24] Yet the debt stayed worryingly high.[25]

How about supermajority processes, notably in the Senate, as a suspect? That case does not work, either. Federal budgets enjoy the luxury of majority rule. The reconciliation procedure of the Budget and Impoundment Act of 1974 rules out filibustering against budgets. Presidents and party majorities are aware of this huge hole in the supermajority dike, and they routinely take advantage of it. In budget terms, perhaps the system is not supermajoritarian enough, as Lawrence Summers has written: "There should have been more checks and balances in place before the huge tax cuts of 1981, 2001 and 2003 [all helped by reconciliation], or to avert the many unfunded entitlement expansions of the past few decades. Most experts would agree that it is a good thing that politics thwarted the effort to establish a guaranteed annual income in the late 1960s and early 1970s and the effort to put in place a 'single-payer' healthcare system during the 1970s."[26]

Is Congress in an overall sense, as compared with the presidency, to draw that particular comparison, a fiscal culprit? That is a surprisingly under-investigated question. It is difficult to address. Theory and street-corner suspicion point to a yes. Distributive politics as conducted in the committees can be profligate.[27] Certainly the congressional budget process in our era, with its opaque omnibus bills and disorienting ten-year sunsets, is no prize.[28] Vision and responsibility are scarcer on Capitol Hill than they might be. But factual backing for this indictment of Congress does not jump out. A different pattern seems to prevail—or at least it did in Paul E. Peterson's careful analysis in 1985 of the eight presidencies of the post–World War II era through Reagan's first term (no one seems to have done a corresponding update): On average, "if the president finds a way of keeping expenditures and revenues roughly in balance, Congress does little to disturb the equilibrium. But if the president insists on major new expenditures or significant tax reductions, Congress is also willing to acquiesce, even if this may mean budget deficits. In short, on overall fiscal policy Congress is not so much responsible as deferential."[29] In sync with this judgment, R. Douglas Arnold wrote in an analysis in 1990: "The result is that Congress enacts fiscal policies that appear remarkably similar to those which presidents propose."[30]

If congressional deference is the norm, it matters what the presidents do.[31] What do they do? In one study, the especially "strong independent" presidents of 1789 through the 1980s were found to excel at curbing fiscal "inefficiencies"—not the same thing as fiscal "imbalances," but suggestive.[32] At the balance task, the presidents have varied. In a 2009 book, Iwan Morgan argues that certain recent presidents have shown a high concern for fiscal balance—Carter, George H. W. Bush, Clinton. Others have been more relaxed—Reagan, George W. Bush.[33] Through 2015 at least, Obama seemed to be rather relaxed. His juices ran to other causes. In general, differing policy effects seem to have ensued from the differing presidential bents.

Budget guardianship or hawkishness seems to be required of the presidents, at least on average. But in political terms, that is a tough role, asking as it does for electoral sacrifice by the presidents or their parties. It was politically risky for Hoover to provoke a large tax hike in 1932, or Eisenhower to forego pump-priming of the economy, or Carter to break with his party's spenders on jobs and health care, or George H. W. Bush to promote the budget deal of 1990 raising taxes (so much for his "Read my lips" pledge), or Clinton to generate the budget deal of 1993 that raised taxes again (a significant minus in the 1994 midterm elections).[34] In earlier times, against heavy interest-group pressure, all four presidents after World War I—Harding, Coolidge, Hoover, and FDR—vetoed budget-busting veterans' bonus bills, although not all the vetoes stuck.[35]

It is a decent bet that at least two presidents since World War II have lost the White House for their parties by insisting on fiscal constraint from Congress and getting it. Eisenhower, one of them, might have nudged the economy just enough to elect Nixon his successor in 1960 if he had acceded to spending pressure from congressional Democrats, then the majority, during his second term.[36] Nixon himself saw the lack of a stimulus nudge as critical. Unemployment, he lamented, was too high during the election season of 1960: "All the speeches, television broadcasts, and precinct work in the world could not counteract that one hard fact."[37] Clinton in 2000, if he had agreed to tax cuts that the House Republican majority was pressing for, rather than, as he did, guard a then-existent budget surplus so as to "save Social Security," might have nudged the economy just enough to elect Al Gore his successor. A judgment by Larry M. Bartels and John Zaller goes, "Clinton may have displayed more fiscal discipline than political sense in spurning Republican proposals for a tax cut."[38] These elections of 1960 and 2000 were knife-edge close. By the customary logic of econometrics, spending or tax-cut jolts of whatever origin might have reversed them.

All this having been said about those two elections, there is a twist. Yes, both the congressional Democrats of the late 1950s and the House Republicans of 2000 seem to have been acting against the electoral interests of the presidential wings of their own parties. But there is an aroma of position taking. The matter is complicated. These congressional parties could win immediate points for the fiscal-imbalancing positions they took, but they could perhaps also expect the incumbent presidents to guard the Treasury and thus incidentally forego for their successor nominees Nixon and Gore the electoral benefits of short-term economic stimulus jolts. At the time, both Eisenhower and Clinton were term-limited and retiring.

Possibly Congress taken alone does indeed lean somewhat toward fiscal imbalance. The evidence is not clear cut. Arnold, in his careful analysis in 1990, was unconvinced. Congress does after all have some of its own guardian instincts and processes.[39] Certainly such instincts and processes were there in earlier days, as is recounted in Richard F. Fenno Jr.'s 1966 work *The Power of the Purse*.[40] But the presidents are there too—as fiscal target setters and, at least some of them, tackers toward fiscal equilibrium.

7

Legitimacy, Messiness, and Reflections

So much for the one-by-one presentations of the thirteen "impulses." They run from Alexander Hamilton's time through Barack Obama's. They run from the country's launch through its mid-nineteenth-century consolidation, from the economic growth zoom of the late nineteenth century through Progressive reform and the New Deal. An ornate welfare state and U.S. international hegemony swing into place. A quest for unexampled prosperity, a civil rights revolution, and a wave of neoliberalism invest the country in the decades after World War II. Then come the current preoccupations of climate change and fiscal disorder. All these impulses have had transnational predicates. What are we to make of them? See table 4 for some judgments regarding them.

Column one in table 4 lists the impulses. Column two places the thirteen U.S. performances in transnational perspective. I will not dwell on the comparative judgments that I offer in this figure. I devised the transnational comparisons so as to provide a yardstick, not for their own sake. In some of the cases the United States has performed distinctively, but the causation for that is complicated, sometimes entailing this country's helpful size, natural wealth, and location as much as its formal institutions. U.S. economic growth and foreign-policy success have pretty obviously profited from those features, not to mention an absence of powerful, aggressive nations next door.

Table 4. U.S. Performance regarding the Thirteen Impulses

The impulse	U.S. record compared with other countries	Chief lever of policy change (executive or Congress)	Nature of executive imprint	Nature of congressional imprint
Launch of new nation	Superior	Executive	Economic stability and growth	System legitimation
Continental expansion	Typical (more or less)	Varied by topic	Acquisition of land	Distribution of land
Mid-19th century consolidation	Unusually violent; typical in some results	Executive	Policy leadership, military muscle, domination by North	Harmonizer across sections, then support of war
Building an industrial economy	Out front (for lots of reasons)	Congress?	Guardian of the currency, domestic order	Tariff and other distributive policies
Taming corporations and the rich	Unusual, but on the mark in its way	Congress	Follow Congress, occasionally lead	Progressive regulatory and tax regimes via lawmaking
Rise to world power	Out front (for lots of reasons)	Executive	Imperial outreach, new role of world hegemon	Lean toward insularity, leeriness of commitments
Responding to the Great Depression	Typical (more or less)	Executive	Monetary shakeup, reform of institutions	Lean toward inflation, spending
Building a welfare state	Smaller, more private	Shared	Big-ticket innovations	Continual increments, a private-side bent

Post–World War 2 prosperity	Out front (for lots of reasons)	Shared; an executive edge	Keynesian management regime	Coauthor of various developmental legislation
Civil rights revolution	Typical timewise, although U.S. context different	Executive and courts	New statutory and administrative regime	Harmonized regional conflict but then legitimated new laws in 1964–65
Neoliberalizing the economy	U.S. initiating role, but commonality of result	Shared, probably an executive edge	New neoliberal policy regime	New neoliberal policy regime
Addressing climate change	U.S. a bit of a laggard lately	Once Congress, now the executive	Policy leadership by Democrats recently	Paced the action in 1960s and 1970s, now laggard
Containing debt and deficit	Typical	Executive	Often tends toward guardian role	On balance more relaxed about the problems

Certain cases offer special U.S. wrinkles that I have discussed—the country's taxation, regulatory, and welfare-state regimes, for example, and its relative lack of colonies. In many cases, however, the U.S. performance has been transnationally generic or close to that, offering little help for upside or downside readings of American distinctiveness or exceptionalism. Perhaps my analytic frame was rigged against finding much U.S. exceptionalism anyway, given the necessarily transnational character of any impulse for it to make it onto the list in the first place. But there we are. There is a good deal of typicality or genericness.

On to column three, which tracks whether Congress or the executive has been the chief lever of policy change. The scoring here is mixed and messy, but on balance the executive comes out ahead. This is not a surprise. Presidents ordinarily supply the initiative in the American system. This question about chief lever comes to mind quickly, but it is not my main concern here. We might also examine, for example, *non*-levering—Santo Domingo doesn't get annexed, civil rights bills don't clear the Senate, veterans' bonuses draw White House vetoes, the White House loses its Indochina war funding, Obama doesn't tackle Syria. Of ultimate interest here are *the distinctive imprints* of the two government branches, in particular Congress, regarding these various performances. For these assessments, see column four (the executive) and column five (Congress). As suggested earlier, many of these institutional juxtapositions do not have a cleanly one-versus-the-other cast. Often the two institutions have clashed, but sometimes they have just left different marks.

As for Congress taken alone, it is not easy to snapshot it in isolation if one's concern is the performance of the whole U.S. government versus the performances of governments elsewhere. Often, as in national budgeting, what cries out for comparison elsewhere is the end result of complex complementarities between Congress and the presidency.

It is hard to generalize across these thirteen congressional performances. Looking across the two and a quarter centuries, I come away impressed by the system's flexibility, its variety, its capacity to surprise—sometimes to turn on a dime. Who would have predicted Congress's passion for progressive taxation a century ago or its lunge into environmental regulation in the 1970s? Aren't legislative bodies supposed to be sluggish and pork-minded? But then there are other proclivities. The whats and whys of the thirteen treatments shoot off in all directions, they open a diversity of speculation, and I will not try to direct them all into a tidy "so what" analysis here at the close. Let each treatment speak for itself. Yet I finish with two general themes. They hark back to my introductory chapter. They do not cover everything, but they do embrace at least many of the thirteen congressional performances. Then I offer some general reflections.

Legitimacy

The first theme is legitimacy. As noted earlier, the American regime has been notably stable, and, by plausible inference anyway, its stability indexes its popular legitimacy. What has been Congress's role in this record? I like an argument offered by the comparativists Matthew Shugart and John Carey: Presidential systems with assemblies that enjoy strong constitutional legislative powers tend to be especially stable. The American system is one of those. In transnational comparison, it is a high-side outlier. Congress has powerful prerogatives. American presidents cannot directly introduce bills, may see their legislative ideas amended (except for treaties) or just plain ignored, have no special constitutional advantage in budgeting, lack a line-item veto, cannot do end runs around Congress by calling popular referenda, and, by cross-national standards anyway, pretty much lack decree powers. Constitutionally, the U.S. presidential system is rather different from most of those in Latin America, the chief homeland of presidencies.

All this can be a boon, Shugart and Carey argue, for long-term system stability. That is because "[a]n assembly represents the diversity of a polity far better than an executive dependent on the president's whims is likely to do." Strong assemblies can stare down rambunctious or sectarian presidents. We have seen both of those kinds in the United States, and we may see more. Idiosyncrasy, petulance, and a take-all-the-marbles arrogance can invest a presidential office. In presidential systems, ideologues, pied pipers, and would-be caudillos can buck for the top jobs. Assemblies can unquestionably act up, too, but as a generality, Shugart and Carey argue, they can "serve as arenas for the perpetual fine-tuning of conflicts. . . . [They have] the potential for encompassing divergent viewpoints and striking compromises on them."[1] In the course of all this—these authors do not dwell on the point—assemblies can excel at weighing voter intensities and blending them into packages. These various services, the argument goes, unlovely as they may loom in day-to-day performance, can be a help to legitimizing a system across a heterogeneous public.

This seems like a story about the United States, which can be eruptively heterogeneous and intensity-prone. Does a case for legitimation pan out? I believe so. I weave a two-part argument. First, I take up the joint topic of race and North-South relations, which has offered by far the most explosive antagonism of American history. In doing this, I pick up previous threads of discussion from chapters 2 and 5. Second, I consider the more general picture of congressional decision making.

Never before has the country been so polarized, we hear these days. This is a bizarre claim. Have we forgotten the 1850s through the 1870s? In the 1850s the sectional sides drifted toward killing each other—then they killed each other. The Civil War brought some 750,000 war deaths, which would be about 7.5 million deaths as a share of the population today.[2] It is hard to get more polarized than that. And afterwards, spirited guerrilla warfare carried on in the South in the late 1860s and 1870s.[3] True, the antagonism of those three decades was chiefly sectional rather than partisan, but in general analytic terms it is best to step back and see party-versus-party conflict, the absorbing theme of today's politics, as just a special case of polarization. Why key on just the parties? At any rate, by a plausible common-sense standard, today's antagonisms are minor compared with those of the mid-nineteenth century. (For that matter, to reach for times in the memories of some of us, how about the polarizing antagonisms of the McCarthy era or the Vietnam era?)

Before the Civil War, Congress bridged the two sections—more accurately, the whites of the two sections. It was a white man's country. The Missouri Compromise of 1820 and the Compromise of 1850 led the congressional performance. In my earlier discussion I cast this action as a response to the nation's median voter, which in theory seems a decent enough interpretation where two sides exist, where they match in numbers and intensity and where moderates are available in the politics too. Harking to the median voter is a plausible first approximation for the behavior of assemblies.

But then, heading into the 1870s, intensity politics took a new form in Congress. More specifically, a pattern of *asymmetric intensity* entered the scene.

A theoretical excursus is in order. In fact, representative assemblies do indeed violate the views of the median voter, at least on secondary matters, insofar as the median voter possesses relevant views, and they do it all the time.[4] We expect assemblies to do that. That is one reason for having assemblies. Assertion butts up against indifference, and assertion wins. Most of us applaud some violations of this sort and deplore others. The sugar industry gets this, the unions get that, New York City gets a bankruptcy bailout (it happened in 1975), multicultural preferences get anchored into law (a hard sell to a state referendum electorate), Nevada stops nuclear waste from getting dumped into its moonlike backyard (the state's senators take care of that). In an assembly, such results can be executed by strenuousness, by persuasion, and, perhaps most interestingly in a theoretical sense, by explicit or implicit logrolling. Pet enterprises can be logrolled into one enactment or, by way of understandings among politicians, across separate enactments. In each of the particular provisions, the median voter may lose out, but the full content of an enactment, or beyond that the full content of a legislative season, may pass muster.

But those are secondary, so to speak, instances of asymmetric intensity. The primary instance in American and congressional history, the one that once dwarfed or underlay a good deal else in the course of the history, has been the gap over race between the North and the white South from the 1870s to the 1960s. The white South, it seemed, had to be appeased. Congress was in the middle of it all. It was Congress that arranged the procedure for, and then accommodated the terms of, the so-called Compromise of 1877.[5] That high-stakes deal settled the disputed Hayes-Tilden presidential election of 1876 by, among other things, ceding the state governments of the Deep South, for generations to come as it turned out, to white "Redeemer" Democrats. Not that any alternative future for those states, given the context of the mid-1870s, had long arms of likelihood, but there we are. The equal rights of the new Fourteenth Amendment and the voting rights of the new Fifteenth Amendment were eroding away in the South.

The Compromise of 1877 shared features with those of 1820 and 1850, but it differed in a key respect. Intensity asymmetry had arrived. Now, a dogged South faced a weary North. That set the terms for a long future. It was at least a congressional process story. Soon, as discussed in chapter 5, the Senate switched into its filibuster mode as a way of accommodating, to put a theoretical spin on the matter, the sectional intensity gap. The southerners put their many feet down. In contests for Senate agenda space, civil rights kept losing out to other issues that the North's senators considered more important—in the 1930s, for example, economic recovery.[6] After 1875, no civil rights laws were enacted until 1957, and the enforcement of existing ones fell off.[7] During that span, it is a plausible bet that the national median voter kept favoring at least some basic civil rights protection in the South, but to little avail. Finally, the Senate's special naysaying role came to an end once pro–civil rights public opinion evolved and Congress came to enact the Voting Rights Act in 1965. There is a milestone comment. The state that had once led the southern secession figures in it. "Don't ask me to go out there and filibuster," remarked Senator Ernest Hollings of South Carolina in the Senate cloakroom five years later. Hollings, a Democrat, had recently won election thanks to African American votes. "I'm not going back to my state and explain a filibuster against the black voters."[8]

Did the Senate's filibuster processes keep *causing* the southern state of affairs during that long time span? We need to be cautious. Military occupation was needed to police the South to a precarious cross-racial civil rights norm under President Grant during Reconstruction, and, after a long era of federal government hands off, military intervention was needed again under President Eisenhower at the Little Rock schools in 1957. Passing or not passing laws can only go so far. But at the least, the Senate tied a ribbon around the cross-sectional accommodation of those times, and it likely did more than that.

Again, this is a legitimation story—or, more accurately, a re-legitimation story. The country could have split apart. It almost did. Elsewhere, certain other nineteenth-century secessionist moves failed, as in Poland and Hungary, yet the early twentieth century brought a rash of separation successes—Norway from Sweden in 1905 and several new independent states including Ireland in the wake of World War I.[9] As it was, the South came to exhibit well past the Civil War a regional one-party system, a racial caste system, a differentiated labor market, its own memorial days, a special taste in flags, and, surprisingly, as late as the 1990s a trace of a trade discontinuity at the border of the old Confederacy.[10] There was ample grist for Confederate independence. Countries can split apart. Some are splitting apart today.

Today these American sectional divergences have vanished or faded, but in earlier times the project of reunion took work. Arend Lijphart, offering a comparative perspective, has seen it as a venture in "consociationalism" centered in Congress: "After the Civil War, a consociational arrangement developed that gave to the Southern segment a high degree of autonomy and to its leaders a crucial position in decision-making by such means as chairmanships of key congressional committees and the filibuster. The slow progress of civil rights legislation was to a large extent caused by these consociational features that added up to an informal but effective Southern veto power."[11]

This was a tragic history—in formal terms, it featured a deal between A and B at the expense of C. It had a flavor of repressiveness by condominium. It had counterparts around those times in South Africa, where the British-stock population after the close of the Boer War partnered with the secondary Dutch-extraction Boers at the expense of the country's blacks (who were, to be sure, unlike the American case, a population majority), and in the late Habsburg Empire where Germans partnered with the secondary Hungarians at the expense of Slavic and Romanian peasantries.[12] To say the least, the U.S. relegitimation of the late nineteenth century extended only so far into the population. For much of the rest there was repression.

I have dwelt on this North-versus-South story owing to its mesh of importance and singularity. It stands by itself. But the case for Congress as legitimizer has a more general cast. It makes for a quite different part two of the argument here. It pervades the history back to the 1790s.

It is this. In regard to particular policies, a good bet for legitimizing them with the public is to enact them in the first place by large legislative majorities or, perhaps even better, majorities that include significant elements of both parties. Ample collections of interests can thus be brought on board. Also, a logic goes, any upfront losers, notably the parties, are in consequence somewhat disabled in subsequent years from possible carping or sabotage as the policies are executed. This disablement idea is under-studied.[13] At any rate, enactments with such broad initial support are well represented in the thirteen treatments in this study. The bent for accommodation that Shugart and Carey discuss jumps out.

Best anchored of all, perhaps, are settlements that majorities of both parties agree to on final passage as they are enacted, such as the Social Security Act of 1935, Medicare in 1965 (at least in the

House), and the elaborately engineered Civil Rights Acts of 1964 and 1965. In the case of Medicare, a hot polarizing issue in its time, the ruling Democrats in 1965 went out of their way to curry buy-in Republican support even though they enjoyed their own large majorities on Capitol Hill.[14] Enactments like these have lived on deeply embedded. In a step down, enactment coalitions that comprised at least some significant cross-party mix dominated the "taming corporations and the rich" drive of the late nineteenth and early twentieth centuries. That includes the historic switch to progressive taxation during 1909–1918, which, taking into account the genesis of the Sixteenth Amendment, enjoyed the signatures of both parties. President Taft, for one, backed the new amendment. The infrastructure moves of the 1950s, the environmental reforms of the 1960s and 1970s, and the neoliberalism of the 1970s and 1980s had a cross-party texture. Thus also the budget deals of 1981, 1985, 1990, 1997, 2011, 2013, and 2015—not to mention the TARP bailout of the financial industry following the Wall Street crash in 2008.[15] As for divided party control of the government in formal terms, key measures enacted in that context have ranged from the Jay Treaty in 1796 through the Interstate Commerce Act in 1887, the Norris–La Guardia Act of 1932, the Marshall Plan to aid a war-ruined Europe in 1948, the Interstate Highway Act of 1956, the Clean Air Act of 1970, the Reagan tax cuts of 1981, the Americans with Disabilities Act of 1990, and welfare reform in 1996.

Enactments crafted in these capacious ways have tended to stick. Hostilities or qualms regarding them have tended to fade. They score points for the idea of legitimation in a sense specific to the policies but also in a sense general to the system. Laws enacted otherwise can run into trouble. Thus notably in recent years, notwithstanding its long-sought policy benefits, the Affordable Care Act of 2010.

Obamacare went to the statute books enjoying zero support from Congress's opposition party in a context of edgy processes and luke-warm, at best, public opinion polls. A ragged policy embedment, voter backlash, a six-year plateau of disappointing polls, and endless opposition carping to the point of sabotage have ensued.[16]

This legitimacy argument is incomplete. To clinch it would require a study of congressional *inaction,* which I have not empha-sized here. Unquestionably, Congress, whatever else may be said about it, has often been very good at inaction. *Deadlock, gridlock, stalemate,* and *stasis* are the familiar terms of description. Change the proper nouns and a James MacGregor Burns statement of 1963 might find traction at many times: "We are mired in governmental dead-lock, as Congress blocks or kills not only most of Mr. Kennedy's bold proposals of 1960, but many planks of the Republican platform as well."[17] For one thing, taking it from the White House standpoint, all the presidents starting with FDR in 1937, possibly excepting Lyndon Johnson, have seen some of their favorite policy initiatives sink on Capitol Hill.[18] That result is, well, routine. It is what you might expect in the sort of institutional design discussed by Shugart and Carey.

Note that inaction as well as action can be legitimizing, although the topic is murky. Often, when confronted by a polarized, dissonant, or irresolute public the unsurprising behavior of a representative assembly is to do nothing at all. Often, when Congress is doing noth-ing at all, to the despair of partisans, intellectuals, and the media, it is actually responding to an unresolved electorate with a perfect ear.[19] *Don't!* the public is in effect collectively saying. Consider a stark coun-terfactual: Every quick, narrow, temporary majority gets to jam into law whatever its activist base wants. Play that out for awhile, espe-cially in a context of ideological polarization, and what level of system legitimacy would result?

Messiness

The second closing theme is the striking messiness of congressional activity. Inconstancy, incoherence, and particularism have invested many public projects. Those bents figure in the country's distributive policy regimes that appear so prominently in column five of table 4. This is trademark congressional stuff. It goes way back.

Often on exhibit is a special flavor of preference aggregation: Congress takes the lead in supplying long-running streams of felicity in small or moderate-sized doses to individuals or groups who clamor for it or at least appreciate it, paying the way in costs that are diffuse or hidden or delayed. Thus the nineteenth-century land distribution regime (I was especially struck by this), the Civil War pensions, the traditional tariff, the interwar veterans' bonuses, and incremental entitlements expansion (as with Congressman Waxman and Medicaid). Tax expenditures would fit the list of such perpetual deliveries of discrete benefits.[20] One-time deference to silver interests might.

What can one say about this brand of policymaking? On the one hand, it can look (and be) dubious. It smacks of ad hoc raids on the public domain, the consumer (as with tariff duties), the taxpayer, or future generations. It can feature constant Capitol Hill tinkering and small regard for administrability. From the standpoint of synoptic policy planning, it is a nightmare. Congress is the natural enemy of those who prefer rationalistic tidiness. In the words of Martha Derthick: "Constantly changing in composition, torn always between its roles as policymaker for the nation and representative of particular constituencies and constituents, responsive by nature to a society that continually changes, Congress engages endlessly in lawmaking. And in doing so, it displays little independent interest in anticipating the administrative consequences of its enactments."[21] Between 1935 and 1990, there were some ninety-two changes in Social Security benefit calculations.[22] As of 2001, there were at least fifteen kinds of federally guaranteed student loans: "Over the years, loan types had proliferated, as Congress sought to fine-tune the loan process."[23] Student loan provision in its programmatic dynamics over time, as in generating and then palliating debt, has been taking on some of the aspects of nineteenth-century land distribution.

On the other hand, the U.S. governing system has no doubt bought retail legitimacy with benefit streams like these. What would life have been like without them? And it is not clear that the overall effects have been all that malign. The farm lands did get settled, the government's occasional bows to silver that did actually occur might have been a net plus, veterans' bonuses were apparently a fiscal plus as well as a much-needed one-on-one blessing in the 1930s, and so on. "Minorities rule," Robert A. Dahl wrote in his classic inductive interpretation of American democracy.[24] Here are some minorities that have ruled. At any rate, there has been a certain containment of the distributive propensity—often supplied by the executive branch, though sometimes by Congress itself. The final profiles of these policy regimes have reflected the felicities of *both* their distribution *and* their containment. An assessment is thus complicated.

Given Congress's bent for messiness, it has been hard to build instrumental rationality of a Weberian style into federal agencies—at least in domestic policy areas. As reviewed earlier, the country's relatively small and late welfare state may be one result, at least partly. The exceptional privateness of the country's economy may be another result, at least partly. The United States has had relatively little experience with government ownership. Here is the speculation (evidence of non-events is hard to come by). Seldom has it seemed a promising idea to allow organizational units hinging on production or productivity within an arm's length of Congress's propensity for servicing constituents and interest groups and its constant tinkering. Regulate the firms, but don't try to own or operate them. Congressional experience with U.S. Post Office politics would seem to fortify this advice. In Richard F. Fenno Jr.'s classic 1973 account, the "first strategic premise" of the House's Post Office Committee members back when the government directly ran the organization was "to support maximum pay increases and improvements in benefits for employee groups and to oppose all rate increases for mail users."[25] It pays to read that statement twice. Once, just after World War I, the government came close to permanent ownership of the railroads European-style. But it drew back. One misgiving was an expected exposure of a government unit to labor union influence.[26] In general, in this circuitous way, Congress through its history might have been a boon for private capitalism.

Reflections

How about Congress today? It is probably wise not to get too tangled in current events. Headlines come and go quickly. But here are some areas discussed earlier. In handling deficits and debt, looking to the mix of policy performance supplied by Congress and the executive, the United States does not seem to be underperforming its peers elsewhere notwithstanding the often weird optics—government shutdowns and the rest. In comparative terms, climate change offers a less favorable picture, yet that may reflect cross-country differences in public opinion. In these areas at least, it is hard to see any distinctive incapacity attaching to the U.S. separation-of-powers system. Long-term pension problems, for one thing, seem to loom *worse* in Europe, with its many parliamentary systems, than in the United States.[27] In recent times, Congress's own particular leanings toward inflation and running up the debt—which have made appearances in history—

have been moderate, containable, or no more culpable than the propensities of the executive.

Doing as well as peer nations may be a low bar. Absolute is not the same as relative. But it is well to take a look elsewhere. Peer countries are having governing problems, too. The other large G8 democracies, beyond their fiscal difficulties, are being afflicted by flat or rigid economies, immigration dilemmas, and identity crises—as in England's ties to Scotland coming unraveled.

Managing conflict seems to be bringing the United States its chief difficulties these days, not just managing particular policies. Polarization has been surging, not to the levels of the 1860s or perhaps other past times, but even so. In a context of a public's polarization there is no easy solution for a representative assembly. To accommodate diverse voter preferences through either action or inaction becomes especially tough. The elected officials can get hammered if they do— as with passing the Affordable Care Act—or hammered if they don't—as with not passing immigration reform.

Fractionalization may be as apt a term as *polarization*. In recent decades, the electoral sphere of the United States has become more *inclusive* at the same time it has become more *heterogeneous*—adding on diversities to the country's already ample historical stock of them. The country's politics is greatly more inclusive today than it used to be. Reasonably comprehensive voter suffrage, by the standards of the developed world, has come to the United States late. How might we measure that inclusiveness? In comparative analysis, one measure of inclusiveness clocks the percentage of any country's total resident population that casts votes in its top-ranking national election.[28] That fraction may seem odd. Babies as well as non-citizens and everybody else figure in the denominator. But the measure offers a solution of sorts to the question: What, in basic analytic terms, in gauging a country's political participation rate at any time, should be the denominator? Forget about legal eligibility. Scope to the full population. In casting back at earlier American times, to use this measure means including in the denominator for calculation purposes, among other people, the country's once enslaved population, also its later de facto disfranchised African American population, and always its women. For any election year in history, the numerator is the total popular vote cast for president; the denominator is the total number of human beings resident on the country's soil at the time. The result is an interesting counterfactual that embraces the whole history. The vaunted nineteenth-century United States comes to look pretty nonparticipatory.

By this standard, the clear winner for the most inclusive presidential election in U.S. history is that of 2008 sending Barack Obama to the White House. (Second prize goes to the Bush-Kerry election of 2004.) Charles A. Kromkowski has done the calculations.[29] The Voting Rights Act of 1965 is one obvious cause of this new inclusiveness. Black mobilization, southern white countermobilization, plus national issue evolution on many matters in sync with the voter expansion have all played roles. The African American rise has been gradual. Directly as regards Congress, the Congressional Black Caucus moved into major player status in the 1990s, historically broadening the inclusivity of the House of Representatives and widening that body's issue profile.[30]

Inclusive representation of a heterogeneous public is an adventure. America's racial division, in its traditional white and black strain—Europe offers no clear analogue to this—is just the beginning in today's scene of expression and fractionalization. Evolving American demography, as in Hispanic and Asian immigration, has brought new issue dimensions. Age, bracketed by the newly constitutionalized eighteen-year-old vote and the growing ranks of senior citizens, has blossomed as a conflict source. Disagreements rage in the electorate centering on gender, trade, class (witness the 2016 presidential primaries of both parties), sexual orientation (a wholly new public issue), multiculturalism versus its opposite, and nationalism versus internationalism or globalism (a tough matter for a country of traditionally fierce nationalism). Intense American differences over guns, abortion, criminal punishment, and secularism versus religiosity do not have much in the way of European analogues. The U.S. establishments, whatever they may be, are under siege in both parties. The left and right, from their colonies of culture and money, face off against each other. Ideologues on all sides brim with certitudes and demands. Failing all else, there is always region—the Confederate flag still flies, albeit less often of late. In short supply is a sense of respect and empathy, which might be an expectation in a civil society, that extends across the country's vast range of interests and tastes.

Managing this inclusive heterogeneity is a task and a half. All the interests and tastes end up in Congress. There, they jangle. They bring haggling, raucousness, showdowns, and the familiar rest. Often, they emanate in deadlock, stalemate, gridlock, and that familiar rest. No center may hold. These days, no common animations of the sort that drew on many of the impulses that I dwell on in this book seem to be inspiriting the American government, or those of peer OECD countries.

In the United States, a customary way out of a congressional morass like this is presidential leadership. That can mean moral leadership, which is best administered in nonsectarian doses. It differs from hectoring. Second, it can mean White House legislative leadership, in foul as well as fair political weather. Virtually all the presidents at least since Hoover (I had no luck squeezing President Ford into the generalization) have reached across the partisan aisles—they needed congressional support from the other side—to clinch at least some measures that they really wanted. Thus Hoover (tax hikes in 1932), FDR (the military draft as World War II approached), Truman (the Marshall Plan), Eisenhower (trade in 1955), Kennedy (to reform the House Rules Committee in 1961), Johnson (civil rights in 1964 and 1965), Nixon (revenue sharing in 1972), Carter (his energy package in 1978), Reagan (tax cuts in 1981), George H. W. Bush (the Clean Air Act of 1990), Clinton (the North American Free Trade Agreement in 1993, welfare reform in 1996), George W. Bush (No Child Left Behind), and Obama (the major budget deals of 2011–15). Skill in congressional maneuvering is a key item in the White House job description. It always has been. Presidents need to relish it and to know how to do it. Coalitions, sometimes odd ones, need to be coddled and built. Congress, to operate effectively, often needs such sensitive intrusion.

On matters involving complex policies, a third recourse to presidential leadership lies in intentional delegation of authority to the executive. This is a dense, vexed topic that I don't want to get into except to say the following. Delegation is an obvious governing need in modern times, but, for reasons of system legitimacy, it is best achieved through congressional statutes that specify reasonably clearly what is being delegated on what terms. This is a constitutional substitute for letting presidents wing it and do whatever they want.

Fortunately, there exists a long U.S. tradition of delegating such authority in response to whatever the times seem to call for, with reasonable success. A template for action is available. Thus, in historic moves, Congress delegated authority to the executive in the Budget and Accounting Act of 1921 creating the Budget Bureau, the Reciprocal Trade Act of 1934 giving leeway to forge trade agreements (augmented in the Trade Reform Act of 1974), the Executive Reorganization Act of 1939 allowing bureaucratic reshuffles, the previously discussed Employment Act of 1946, and the National Security Act of 1947 spiffing up central control on that front. Sometimes the delegation can be breathtaking, as in Congress's statutory messages to the executive in 1917 and 1941 as the world wars set in, saying more or less "please win these wars." By a familiar statutory device, the presidency can be given ad hoc fast-track authority—that is, regarding White House proposals in a specified area, a pathway to future congressional action uncluttered by filibusters or amendments. That device has been employed chiefly on trade, but I see no reason why it couldn't be employed much more widely if need be.

Congress can also put its feet down, taking authority back or saying to the White House that enough is enough.[31] Thus, for example, the Budget and Impoundment and Control Act of 1974 that clipped a Nixon-era practice of impounding congressionally appropriated money and created the Congressional Budget Office (CBO) to rival White House budgetary power. Beyond all this, there exists a sophisticated statutory tradition of, to cite certain major examples, routinizing the activities of the executive branch so as to insure fair treatment in administration, overseeing those activities by congressional committee, making the activities more transparent, and stationing something like moles within the executive branch. The relevant statutes are, respectively, the Administrative Procedure Act of 1946, the Legislative Reorganization Act of 1946, the Freedom of Information Acts (FOIA) of 1967 and 1974, and the Inspector General Act of 1978.[32]

This is a mouthful of instances, but there is a mouthful of history. The point is this. There exists a long, flexible, accordion-like tradition of delegating authority to the executive branch—and sometimes undelegating it—through the considered passage of congressional statutes that help legitimize those moves. That is the way to go. If the executive branch needs to be rendered more powerful, which sometimes it does, this is the way to do it.

Action like this stops short of enabling an all-purpose White House leviathan. Unlimited, take-all-the-marbles power at the top seems a bad idea for a heterogeneous society like today's United States. It is well to remember that the designers of the U.S. Constitution tailored that document to a signally heterogeneous society. "Factions," whether comprised of majorities or minorities, in James Madison's classic formulation in *Federalist* 10, could be a threat to the system. Very happily, today's heterogeneities aren't the same as those back then in the days of slavery. But our own versions do jam today's political context. For that reason and others, it is probably wise to preserve Congress's lusty constitutional powers to check and balance—that is, to legislate, to supply funds, to investigate, and to sound off.

Notes

Introduction

1. Two recent works on the undemocratic features of the U.S. Constitution give major attention to Congress: Robert A. Dahl, *How Democratic Is the American Constitution?* (New Haven, CT: Yale University Press, 2002); Sanford Levinson, *Our Undemocratic Constitution: Where the Constitution Goes Wrong (And How We the People Can Correct It)* (New York: Oxford University Press, 2008).

2. See Roger H. Davidson, David M. Kovenock, and Michael K. O'Leary, *Congress in Crisis: Politics and Congressional Reform* (Belmont, CA: Wadsworth Publishing Co., 1966), pp. 52–53; John R. Hibbing and Elizabeth Theiss-Morse, *Congress as Public Enemy: Public Attitudes toward American Political Institutions* (New York: Cambridge University Press, 1995), pp. 31–36; Robert H. Durr, John B. Gilmour, and Christina Wolbrecht, "Explaining Congressional Approval," *American Journal of Political Science* 41:1 (January 1997), 175–207, at 178–82; John D. Griffin, "Public Evaluations of Congress," ch. 16 in Eric Schickler and Frances E. Lee (eds.), *The Oxford Handbook of the American Congress* (New York: Oxford University Press, 2011); "Gallup: Congress and the Public," available at www.gallup.com/poll/1600/congress-public.aspx.

3. The critical tradition is discussed in Roger H. Davidson and Walter J. Oleszek, *Congress against Itself* (Bloomington: Indiana University Press, 1977), ch. 1.

4. Woodrow Wilson, *Congressional Government: A Study in American Politics* (Mineola, NY: Dover, 2006; original edition 1885), obstructionist at pp. 69–70, 77, opaque at pp. 70–71, 130–31, particularistic at p. 121, unaccountable at ch. 2 passim and pp. 102, 132, 187, meddlesome at pp. 49–51 and 183–86, debate at pp. 69–79, bad policies at e.g. pp. 89, 128, servile at p. 153.

5. James Bryce, *The American Commonwealth,* vol. 1 (New York: Macmillan 1888), p. 142.

6. Introduction to Wilson, *Congressional Government,* p. 8. See Richard H. Rovere, *Senator Joe McCarthy* (New York: Harcourt, Brace and World, 1959) for a trenchant account.

7. George B. Galloway, *Congress at the Crossroads* (New York: Thomas Y. Crowell, 1946); James MacGregor Burns, *Congress on Trial: The Legislative Process and the Administrative State* (New York: Harper and Brothers, 1949); James MacGregor Burns, *The Deadlock of Democracy: Four-Party Politics in America* (Englewood Cliffs, NJ: Prentice-Hall, 1963); Robert Bendiner, *Obstacle Course on Capitol Hill* (New York: McGraw-Hill, 1964); Joseph S. Clark, *Congress: The Sapless Branch* (New York: Harper and Row, 1964); Davidson, Kovenick, and O'Leary, *Congress in Crisis;* Haynes Johnson and David S. Broder, *The System: The American Way of Politics at the Breaking Point* (Boston: Little, Brown, 1996); Juliet Eilperin, *Fight Club Politics: How Partisanship Is Poisoning the House of Representatives* (Lanham, MD: Rowman and Littlefield, 2006); Thomas E. Mann and Norman J. Ornstein, *The Broken Branch: How Congress Is Failing America and How to Get It Back on Track* (New York: Oxford University Press, 2006).

8. Burns, *Congress on Trial,* terms respectively at pp. xi, 40, 120, 120, 121, 127, 128, 134, 207.

9. See Wilson, *Congressional Government,* for scattered declinist arguments at pp. 28, 44, 49–52, 84–85, 111, 128, 140–41, 205–06.

10. The flavor and the judgment are nicely available in a work written in the midst of that time: William S. White, *Citadel: The Story of the U.S. Senate* (New York: Harper and Brothers, 1957).

11. Mann and Ornstein, *Broken Branch,* pp. 9, 146, 146, 169, 170, 184.

12. As in Thomas E. Mann and Norman J. Ornstein, *It's Even Worse Than It Looks: How the American Constitutional System Collided with the New Politics of Extremism* (New York: Basic Books, 2012), p. xiii.

13. Wilson in *Congressional Government* took issue with many federal government policies: post–Civil War intrusion into the South's elections (pp. 39–40) and jury system (pp. 42–43); the Tenure of Office Act (pp. 51–52); internal improvements (pp. 40, 119–21, 133); tariffs (pp. 100–01, 123–24); extravagant spending (p. 102); running big surpluses (p. 102); Republican plans for federal aid to education (pp. 40–41). All this opposition was the standard Democratic Party line of the time, certainly among southerners but also, generally speaking, the party's northerners too. It is a sure bet that Wilson's dislike of the policies bled into his critique of congressional structure.

14. Mann and Ornstein, *Broken Branch,* pp. 3, 27.

15. A classic statement is Juan J. Linz, "Presidential or Parliamentary Democracy: Does It Make a Difference?" ch. 1 in Juan J. Linz and Arturo Valenzuela (eds.), *The Failure of Presidential Democracy* (Baltimore: John Hopkins University Press, 1994). It is true that Linz sees the particular U.S. system, about which he says little, as an exception to a general cross-national pattern associating presidential systems with instability.

16. See David R. Mayhew, *Partisan Balance: Why Political Parties Don't Kill the U.S. Constitutional System* (Princeton, NJ: Princeton University Press, 2011), ch. 5.

17. See Steven G. Calabresi, "Does Institutional Design Make a Difference?" *Northwestern University Law Review* 109:3 (Spring 2015), 578–99, at 584.

18. On this last point, see David R. Mayhew, "Is Congress 'the Broken Branch'?" *Boston University Law Review* 89:2 (April 2009), 357–69, at 367–69.

Chapter 1. Impulses and Imprints

1. On the executive branch during U.S. history, see for example Keith E. Whittington and Daniel P. Carpenter, "Executive Power in American Institutional Development," *Perspectives on Politics* 1:3 (September 2003), 495–513.

2. Niccolò Machiavelli, *Discourses on the First Decade of Titus Livius,* translated from the Italian by Ninian Hill Thompson (London: BiblioBazaar, 2007; original copyright, 1883), book 1, ch. 4.

3. That is, in the spirit of Thomas Babington Macaulay's classic mid-nineteenth-century work *The History of England from the Accession of James III.* There is an abridged edition: Thomas Babington Macaulay, *The History of England* (London: Penguin, 1979).

4. A classic work in this comparing vein is Lawrence H. Chamberlain, *The President, Congress, and Legislation* (New York: Columbia University Press, 1946).

Chapter 2. Building a State and a Nation

1. R. R. Palmer, *The Age of the Democratic Revolution: A Political History of Europe and America, 1760–1800,* 2 vols. (Princeton, NJ: Princeton University Press, 1959–64).

2. Daniel H. Deudney, "The Philadelphian System: Sovereignty, Arms Control, and Balance of Power in the American States-Union, circa 1787–1861," *International Organization* 49:2 (Spring 1995), 191–228.

3. On the case of Europe, see Charles Tilly, "Reflections on the History of European State-Making," ch. 1 in Charles Tilly (ed.), *The Formation of National States in*

Western Europe (Princeton, NJ: Princeton University Press, 1975); Charles Tilly, *Coercion, Capital, and European States, A.D. 990–1992* (Cambridge, MA: Blackwell, 1992), ch. 2.

4. See Lester D. Langley, *The Americas in the Age of Revolution, 1750–1850* (New Haven, CT: Yale University Press, 1996), ch. 11; Robert E. Gallman, "Economic Growth and Structural Change in the Long Nineteenth Century," ch. 1 in Stanley L. Engerman and Robert E. Gallman (eds.), *The Cambridge Economic History of the United States,* vol. 2, *The Long Nineteenth Century* (New York: Cambridge University Press, 2000), pp. 2–6. Argentina's economy grew faster than this country's in the nineteenth century, although the tiny size of its population at the outset clouds comparison. For a Western Hemisphere comparison, see also Joshua Simon, "The Americas' More Perfect Unions: New Institutional insights from Comparative Political Theory," *Perspectives on Politics* 12:4 (December 2014), 808–28.

5. Richard Sylla, "Financial Foundations: Public Credit, the National Bank, and Securities Markets," ch. 2 in Douglas A. Irwin and Richard Sylla (eds.), *Founding Choices: American Economic Policy in the 1790s* (Chicago: University of Chicago Press, 2011), p. 83.

6. Abolition of slavery was a theme in the British North American colonies and elsewhere during the Enlightenment phase of the eighteenth century, but then the impulse seems to have diminished. This up-and-down trajectory was exemplified in the evolution of Thomas Jefferson's views and actions.

7. Seymour Martin Lipset, *The First New Nation: The United States in Historical and Comparative Perspective* (New York: Basic Books, 1979), pp. 16–23.

8. Ron Chernow, *Alexander Hamilton* (New York: Penguin, 2004), chs. 15–18; Thomas K. McCraw, *The Founders and Finance: How Hamilton, Gallatin, and Other Immigrants Forged a New Economy* (Cambridge, MA: Harvard University Press, 2012), chs. 8–11; Stanley Elkins and Eric McKitrick, *The Age of Federalism: The Early American Republic, 1788–1800,* (New York: Oxford University Press, 1993), pp. 114–31, 146–61, 223–44, ch. 9; Douglas A. Irwin and Richard Sylla, "The Significance of the Founding Choices: Editors' Introduction," pp. 1–21 in Irwin and Sylla (eds.), *Founding Choices*; Richard Sylla, Robert E. Wright, and Donald J. Cowen, "Alexander Hamilton, Central Banker: Crisis Management during the U.S. Financial Panic of 1792," *Business History Review* 83 (Spring 2009), 61–86; Douglas A. Irwin, "Revenue or Reciprocity? Founding Feuds over Early U.S. Trade Policy," ch. 3 in Irwin and Sylla (eds.), *Founding Choices*; Max M. Edling, *A Hercules in the Cradle: War, Money, and the American State, 1783–1867,* (Chicago: University of Chicago Press, 2014), ch. 3.

9. Thomas K. McCraw, "The Strategic Vision of Alexander Hamilton," *The American Scholar* 63:1 (Winter 1994), 31–57, quotation at 32.

10. Sylla, "Financial Foundations," p. 60.

11. On taxes: Max M. Edling, *A Revolution in Favor of Government: Origins of the U.S. Constitution and the Making of the American State* (New York: Oxford University Press, 2003), chs. 13, 14. On entrepreneurialism: McCraw, *Founders and Finance*, pp. 131–32; Peter L. Rousseau and Richard Sylla, "Emerging Financial Markets and Early U.S. Growth," *Explorations in Economic History* 42 (2005), 1–26, at 13, 20–21, quotation p. 2.

12. Gordon S. Wood, *Empire of Liberty: A History of the Early Republic, 1789–1815* (New York: Oxford University Press, 2009), p. 201. On this onset of prosperity, see also Peter H. Lindert and Jeffrey G. Williamson, "American Incomes Before and After the Revolution," *Journal of Economic History* 73:3 (2013), 725–65, at 752; Max M. Edling and Mark D. Kaplanoff, "Alexander Hamilton's Fiscal Reform: Transforming the Structure of Taxation in the Early Republic," *William and Mary Quarterly* 61:4 (October 2004), 713–44, at 740, 742.

13. Irwin and Sylla, "Significance of the Founding Choices," pp. 3–4.

14. On the economy, a discussion of counterfactuals appears in Sylla, "Financial Foundations," pp. 84–86.

15. On the economy, see, for example, Edling, *Hercules in the Cradle*, pp. 14, 87, 107, 116. On the Barbary Wars, see Frank Lambert, *The Barbary Wars: American Independence in the Atlantic World* (New York: Hill and Wang, 2007).

16. Elkins and McKitrick, *Age of Federalism*, pp. 58–64.

17. Kenneth A. Shepsle, "Representation and Governance: The Great Legislative Trade-off," *Political Science Quarterly* 103:3 (Autumn 1988), 461–84, at 465. See also Jeffery A. Jenkins and Charles Stewart III, *Fighting for the Speakership: The House and the Rise of Party Government* (Princeton, NJ: Princeton University Press, 2013), p. 58; Leonard D. White, *The Federalists: A Study in Administrative History* (New York: Macmillan, 1948), pp. 73–74; Nelson W. Polsby, "The Institutionalization of the U.S. House of Representatives," *American Political Science Review* 62:1 (March 1968), 144–68, at 154–55. Norman K. Risjord offers an especially detailed account in "Partisanship and Power: House Committees and the Power of the Speaker, 1789–1801," *William and Mary Quarterly* 49:4 (October 1992), 628–51, at 640–45.

18. White, *Federalists*, pp. 328–30; McCraw, *Founders and Finance*, pp. 200–05, 217; Robert V. Remini, *The House: The History of the House of Representatives* (New York: HarperCollins, 2006), p. 61; Risjord, "Partisanship and Power," 643–44.

19. Elkins and McKitrick, *Age of Federalism,* ch. 9; Jeffrey L. Pasley, *The First Presidential Contest: 1796 and the Founding of American Democracy* (Lawrence: University Press of Kansas, 2013), chs. 3, 4; Todd Estes, *The Jay Treaty Debate, Public Opinion, and the Evolution of Early American Political Culture* (Amherst: University of Massachusetts Press, 2006).

20. John F. Hoadley, *Origins of American Political Parties, 1789–1803* (Lexington: University Press of Kentucky, 1986), p. 137.

21. Good accounts appear in Bruce Ackerman, *The Failure of the Founding Fathers: Jefferson, Marshall, and the Rise of Presidential Democracy* (Cambridge, MA: Belknap Press, 2005), chs. 2–5; John Ferling, *Adams vs. Jefferson: The Tumultuous Election of 1800* (New York: Oxford University Press, 2004), ch. 12; Edward J. Larson, *A Magnificent Catastrophe: The Tumultuous Election of 1800: America's First Presidential Campaign* (New York: Free Press, 2007), ch. 10; Bernard A. Weisberger, *America Afire: Jefferson, Adams, and the Revolutionary Election of 1800* (New York: William Morrow, 2000), pp. 258–77; James Roger Sharp, *The Deadlocked Election of 1800: Jefferson, Burr, and the Union in the Balance* (Lawrence: University Press of Kansas, 2010), chs. 8–10; Joanne B. Freeman, "The Election of 1800: A Study in the Logic of Political Change," *Yale Law Journal* 108:8 (June 1999), 1959–94, at 1963–68.

22. Ackerman, *Failure of the Founding Fathers,* p. 93.

23. Adam Przeworski, "Acquiring the Habit of Changing Governments through Elections," *Comparative Political Studies* 48:1 (2015), 101–29, at 102, 110.

24. Adam Przeworski, *Democracy and the Market: Political and Economic Reforms in Eastern Europe and Latin America* (New York: Cambridge University Press, 1991), p. 10.

25. The Federalists were not exactly a political party before the mid-1790s, but there was a twelve-year continuity in coalitional rule of the executive branch from 1789 into 1801.

26. For the 52% figure, see Ferling, *Adams vs. Jefferson,* p. 170.

27. See Freeman, "Election of 1800," pp. 1964–65.

28. On the world in general: C. A. Bayly, *The Birth of the Modern World, 1780–1914: Global Connections and Comparisons* (Malden, MA: Blackwell, 2004), ch. 12; Jürgen Osterhammel, *The Transformation of the World: A Global History of the Nineteenth Century* (Princeton, NJ: Princeton University Press, 2014), ch. 7; Michael Adas, "From Settler Colony to Global Hegemon: Integrating the Exceptionalist Narrative of the American Experience into World History," *American Historical Review* 106:5 (December 2001), 1692–1720, at 1712–18. On the Anglophone world:

James Belich, *Replenishing the Earth: The Settler Revolution and the Rise of the Anglo-World, 1783–1939* (New York: Oxford University Press, 2009), chs. 3, 4, 8; Paul F. Sharp, "Three Frontiers: Some Comparative Studies of Canadian, American, and Australian Settlement," *Pacific Historical Review* 24:4 (November 1955), 369–77; John McQuilton, "Comparative Frontiers: Australia and the United States," *Australasian Journal of American Studies* 12:1 (July 1993), 26–46; C. D. Rowley, *The Destruction of Aboriginal Society: Aboriginal Policy and Practice,* vol. 1 (Canberra: Australian National University Press, 1970).

29. Belich, *Replenishing the Earth,* pp. 522–29.

30. Rowley, *Destruction of Aboriginal Society,* ch. 3; Belich, *Replenishing the Earth,* ch. 8; Bayly, *Birth of the Modern World,* pp. 439–40.

31. On the Canadians: Sharp, "Three Frontiers," pp. 373–74.

32. Troy Bickham, *The Weight of Vengeance: The United States, the British Empire, and the War of 1812* (New York: Oxford University Press, 2012), ch. 3.

33. On the Louisiana Purchase: D. W. Meinig, *The Shaping of America: A Geographical Perspective on 500 Years of History,* vol 2, *Continental America, 1800–1867* (New Haven, CT: Yale University Press, 1993), pt. 1, ch. 1. On the Gadsden Purchase: John Ashworth, *Slavery, Capitalism and Politics in the Antebellum Republic,* vol. 2, *The Coming of the Civil War, 1850–1861* (New York: Cambridge University Press, 2007), p. 383. On Alaska: Walter Nugent, *Habits of Empire: A History of American Expansion* (New York: Alfred A. Knopf, 2008), pp. 237–51. For Congress, the Alaska purchase was a hard sell.

34. Daniel Walker Howe, *What Hath God Wrought: The Transformation of America, 1815–1848* (New York: Oxford University Press, 2007), pp. 658–72, 677–82, 698–700.

35. Amy S. Greenberg, *A Wicked War: Polk, Clay, Lincoln, and the 1846 U.S. Invasion of Mexico* (New York: Alfred A. Knopf, 2012), chs. 4, 5, 12, 13. On congressional hostility: pp. 260–61.

36. Meinig, *Shaping of America,* vol. 2, pt. 1, chs. 2, 5; Nugent, *Habits of Empire,* ch. 4; Howe, *What Hath God Wrought,* pp. 74–77, 97–111; Walter Johnson, *River of Dark Dreams: Slavery and Empire in the Cotton Kingdom* (Cambridge, MA: Harvard University Press, 2013), ch. 1; David S. Heidler, "The Politics of National Aggression: Congress and the First Seminole War," *Journal of the Early Republic* 13:4 (Winter 1993), 501–30.

37. On Jefferson: Meinig, *Shaping of America,* pp. 79–80; Ronald N. Satz, *American Indian Policy in the Jacksonian Era* (Norman: University of Oklahoma Press,

2002), Jon Meacham, *Thomas Jefferson: The Art of Power* (New York: Random House, 2012), p. 392. On Jackson: Howe, *What Hath God Wrought*, pp. 98–107, 342–57; Satz, *American Indian Policy*, chs. 1, 4.

38. Howe, *What Hath God Wrought*, p. 347. See also Satz, *American Indian Policy*, p. 19.

39. Alfred A. Cave, "Abuse of Power: Andrew Jackson and the Indian Removal Act of 1830," *The Historian* 65:6 (December 2003), 1330–53; Howe, *What Hath God Wrought*, pp. 414–23.

40. Howe, *What Hath God Wrought*, pp. 356–57.

41. Jonathan Martin, "Democrats Sever Ties to Founders of Party: Jefferson-Jackson Dinners Are Renamed," *New York Times*, August 12, 2015, p. A12; Russell Berman, "Is the Democratic Party Abandoning Jefferson and Jackson?" *The Atlantic*, July 28, 2015.

42. See Andrew W. Robertson, "Afterword: Reconceptualizing Jeffersonian Democracy," *Journal of the Early Republic* 33:2 (Summer 2013), 317–34, at 317–21; Stanley L. Engerman and Kenneth L. Sokoloff, "The Evolution of Suffrage Institutions in the New World," *Journal of Economic History* 65:4 (September 2005), 891–921, at 895–909; Donald Ratcliffe, "The Right to Vote and the Rise of Democracy, 1787–1828," *Journal of the Early Republic* 33:2 (Summer 2013), 219–54.

43. Lampi referred to, and quotations at, Ratcliffe, "Right to Vote," p. 220.

44. Some sources on the administration: McCraw, *Founders and Finance*, ch. 12; Malcolm J. Rohrbough, *The Land Office Business: The Settlement and Administration of American Public Lands, 1789–1837* (New York: Oxford University Press, 1968), chs. 2–4, 10, 14. By the 1830s the General Land Office was far from a model of bureaucratic effectiveness. See Daniel P. Carpenter, *The Forging of Bureaucratic Autonomy: Reputations, Networks, and Policy Innovation in Executive Agencies, 1862–1928* (Princeton, NJ: Princeton University Press, 2001), pp. 56–57.

45. A refreshing exception is Michael A. Blaakman, "Speculators and States: Land Mania in the Early American Republic," paper presented at conference on "Taking Stock of the State in Nineteenth-Century America," at the Yale Center for the Study of Representative Institutions, New Haven, Connecticut, April 15–16, 2016. This paper draws from a completed dissertation.

46. James C. Scott, *Seeing Like a State: How Certain Schemes to Improve the Human Condition Have Failed* (New Haven, CT: Yale University Press, 1998), pp. 49–51; Rohrbough, *Land Office Business*, ch. 1; John Opie, *The Law of the Land: Two Hundred Years of American Farmland Policy* (Lincoln: University of Nebraska

Press, 1987), ch. 1; Everett Dick, *The Lure of the Land: A Social History of the Public Lands from the Articles of Confederation to the New Deal* (Lincoln: University of Nebraska Press, 1970), ch. 3.

47. There are several fine sources on the politics of land assignment: Rohrbough, *Land Office Business* (he reports 375 laws passed through 1837, p. 295), passim; Opie, *Law of the Land*, chs. 1–5; Dick, *Lure of the Land*, chs. 1, 2, 5, 8–10; Jeremy Atack, Fred Bateman, and William N. Parker, "Northern Agriculture and the Westward Movement," ch. 7 in Engerman and Gallman (eds.), *The Cambridge Economic History of the United States*, vol. 2, *The Long Nineteenth Century*, at pp. 287–302.

48. On the foregone revenue: McCraw, *Founders and Finance*, p. 251. On the squatters: Rohrbough, *Land Office Business*, pp. 202–03. On the easy credit: Opie, *Law of the Land*, p. 53.

49. Richard Sylla, "Experimental Federalism: The Economics of American Government, 1789–1914," ch. 12 in Engerman and Gallman (eds.), *The Cambridge Economic History of the United States*, vol. 2, *The Long Nineteenth Century*, at p. 515; Nugent, *Habits of Empire*, p. 231; Lance E. Davis et al., *American Economic Growth: An Economist's History of the United States* (New York: Harper and Row, 1972), p. 106.

50. On the slave plantations: Johnson, *River of Dark Dreams*, pp. 31–34; Adam Rothman, *Slave Country: American Expansion and the Origins of the Deep South* (Cambridge, MA: Harvard University Press, 2005), ch. 1. On economic growth: Davis et al., *American Economic Growth*, pp. 105, 654.

51. Graham G. Dodds, *Take Up Your Pen: Unilateral Presidential Directives in American Politics* (Philadelphia: University of Pennsylvania Press, 2013), pp. 72–78, 88, 97–104, 144–50.

52. In general, see E. J. Hobsbawm, *The Age of Capital, 1848–1875* (New York: Scribner's Sons, 1975), p. 1, chs. 4–9.

53. Hobsbawm, *Age of Capital*, ch. 3.

54. For Germany, the case rests on the country's territorial unification, beefed-up central government and citizenship identity, lowered social barriers, new parliament, and expanded suffrage, even if full liberalization fell well short. On Germany, Italy, and Hungary: Hobsbawm, *Age of Capital*, pp. 71–78, 82–83, 88–90, 104–05. (To Hungary came, whatever else, a new quasi-sovereignty and independent parliament resting on Magyar nationalism.) On Japan: Hobsbawm, *Age of Capital*, pp. 83–84, 146–54. On Mexico: Hobsbawm, *Age of Capital*, pp. 119–20; Jan Bazant, "Mexico from Independence to 1867," ch. 10 in Leslie Bethell (ed.), *Cambridge*

History of Latin America, vol. 3, *From Independence to c. 1870* (New York: Cambridge University Press, 1985). On Argentina: John Lynch, "The River Plate Republics from Independence to the Paraguayan War," ch. 15 in Bethell (ed.), *Cambridge History of Latin America,* vol. 3, *From Independence to c. 1870,* at pp. 615–58.

55. On Jewish emancipation in Germany: "When Germany was unified by Bismarck, full citizenship was granted to Jews, first throughout the North German Federation in 1869 and then in the entire Reich in 1871." George M. Fredrickson, *Racism: A Short History* (Princeton, NJ: Princeton University Press, 2002), pp. 76–77. On Germany and the Habsburg realm: Osterhammel, *Transformation of the World,* pp. 144, 871.

56. Deudney draws a comparison between nineteenth-century institutional instability in the United States and, entailing the Concert of Europe, Europe as a whole. "Philadelphian System," 219. "The Concert gradually declined in the middle and later years of the nineteenth century," partly because "the domestic regime types of the members (absolutist monarchical versus constitutional monarchical) lay in opposition, a situation analogous to the slavery conflict in America."

57. Hobsbawm, *Age of Capital,* pp. 182–83.

58. Bayly, *Birth of the Modern World,* pp. 161–65, quotation at 162.

59. Peter Kolchin, "Reexamining Southern Emancipation in Comparative Perspective," *Journal of Southern History* 81:1 (February 2015), 7–40, quotation at 9. See also Peter Kolchin, *Unfree Labor: American Slavery and Russian Serfdom* (Cambridge, MA: Belknap Press, 1990).

60. Deudney, "Philadelphian System," 220. See also Danilo Petranovich, "Lincoln's New Nationalism," in Steven B. Smith (ed.), *The Writings of Abraham Lincoln* (New Haven, CT: Yale University Press, 2012), pp. 437–48.

61. See Eric Foner, *Free Soil, Free Labor, Free Men: The Ideology of the Republican Party before the Civil War* (New York: Oxford University Press, 1970). The second quotation is from Richard Franklin Bensel, *Yankee Leviathan: The Origins of Central State Authority in America, 1859–1877* (New York: Cambridge University Press, 1990), p. 2.

62. See, for example, Gregory P. Downs, *After Appomattox: Military Occupation and the Ends of War* (Cambridge, MA: Harvard University Press, 2015).

63. Hobsbawm emphasizes the wars: *Age of Capital,* ch. 4.

64. The analogy to Bismarck and Cavour: Hobsbawm, *Age of Capital,* p. 4; Carl N. Degler, "One Among Many: The United States and National Unification," ch. 4 in Gabor S. Boritt (ed.) *Lincoln, the War President: The Gettysburg Lectures* (New York:

Oxford University Press, 1992). To Bismarck and Lenin: Edmund Wilson, *Patriotic Gore: Studies in the Literature of the American Civil War* (New York: Oxford University Press, 1962), pp. xvi–xix.

65. Bruce Levine, *The Fall of the House of Dixie: The Civil War and the Social Revolution That Transformed the South* (New York: Random House, 2013).

66. See, for example, Arthur M. Schlesinger Jr., *The Imperial Presidency* (Boston: Houghton Mifflin, 1973), pp. 58–60.

67. On the procedural inventiveness of the Compromise of 1850, see Fergus M. Bordewich, *America's Great Debate: Henry Clay, Stephen A. Douglas, and the Compromise That Preserved the Union* (New York: Simon and Schuster, 2012). Recently, the congressional "fiscal cliff" deal of January 1, 2013, had a similar inventive oddity. On the antebellum era of compromise, see Merrill D. Peterson, *The Great Triumvirate: Webster, Clay, and Calhoun* (New York: Oxford University Press, 1987).

68. See Gerry Mackie, *Democracy Defended* (New York: Cambridge University Press, 2003), ch. 12; Alexander Tabarrok and Lee Spector, "Would the Borda Count Have Avoided the Civil War?" *Journal of Theoretical Politics* 11:2 (1999), 261–88.

69. On Adams: William Lee Miller, *Arguing about Slavery: the Great Battle in the United States Congress* (New York: Alfred A. Knopf, 1996); Daniel Walker Howe, *The Political Culture of the American Whigs* (Chicago: University of Chicago Press, 1979), ch. 3. On Wilmot: Eric Foner, "The Wilmot Proviso Revisited," *Journal of American History* 56 (1969), 262–79. On Sumner: David Donald, *Charles Sumner and the Coming of the Civil War* (New York: Alfred A. Knopf, 1967), pp. 227–39, 254–56, ch. 11, pp. 352–65; Thomas C. Leonard, *The Power of the Press: The Birth of American Political Reporting* (New York: Oxford University Press, 1986), pp. 84–86. On the antislavery campaign in Congress in the 1840s: Corey Brooks, "Stoking the 'Abolition Fire in the Capitol': Liberty Party Lobbying and Antislavery in Congress," *Journal of the Early Republic* 33:3 (Fall 2013), 523–47.

70. Terry L. Seip, *The South Returns to Congress: Men, Economic Measures, and Intersectional Relationships, 1868–1879* (Baton Rouge: Louisiana University Press, 1983), especially ch. 8.

Chapter 3. Surges and Their Constraints

1. Keith T. Poole and Howard Rosenthal, *Ideology and Congress* (New Brunswick, NJ: Transaction, 2007).

2. Charles R. Morris, *The Dawn of Innovation: The First American Industrial Revolution* (New York: Public Affairs, 2012), p. xiii.

3. Morris, *Dawn of Innovation,* quotation at p. 269; Richard Sylla, "Experimental Federalism: The Economics of American Government, 1789–1914," ch. 12 in Stanley L. Engerman and Robert E. Gallman (eds.), *The Cambridge Economic History of the United States,* vol. 2, *The Long Nineteenth Century* (New York: Cambridge University Press, 2000), at 532–34. On the enactment of the Morrill Land Grant College Act of 1862: Williamjames Hull Hoffer, *To Enlarge the Machinery of Government: Congressional Debates and the Growth of the American State, 1858–1891* (Baltimore: Johns Hopkins University Press, 2007), ch. 2. Strictly speaking, Congress enacted the Morrill Tariff in a lame duck session in March 1861 just before the Republicans took over the government, but the anti-protectionist senators from the South were a ragged presence by then.

4. Robert J. Gordon, *The Rise and Fall of American Growth: The U.S. Standard of Living Since the Civil War* (Princeton, NJ: Princeton University Press, 2016), p. 312.

5. Robert Bothwell, *Your Country, My Country: A Unified History of the United States and Canada* (New York: Oxford University Press, 2015), p. 121.

6. David Herbert Donald, *Lincoln Reconsidered: Essays on the Civil War Era,* 3rd ed. (New York: Vintage, 2001), pp. 133–37, quotations at 136, 137. In these policy areas, Heather Cox Richardson emphasizes the role of Congress in *The Greatest Nation of the Earth: Republican Economic Policies during the Civil War* (Cambridge, MA: Harvard University Press, 1997), chs. 4–6.

7. Richardson, *Greatest Nation of the Earth,* chs. 2, 3; Robert P. Sharkey, *Money, Class, and Party: An Economic Study of Civil War and Reconstruction* (Baltimore: Johns Hopkins University Press, 1959), ch. 6.

8. Max M. Edling, *A Hercules in the Cradle: War, Money, and the American State, 1783–1867* (Chicago: University of Chicago Press, 2014), pp. 185–96, 204–15, quotation at p. 205.

9. Morris, *Dawn of Innovation,* pp. 270–71.

10. Stuart Bruchey, *The Wealth of the Nation: An Economic History of the United States* (New York: Harper & Row, 1988), pp. 67–69; see also Morris, *Dawn of Innovation,* pp. 269–72.

11. Morris, *Dawn of Innovation,* p. 272, comparison of the nineteenth-century economic trajectories of Britain and the United States ch. 8. See also Monica Prasad, *The Land of Too Much: American Abundance and the Paradox of Poverty* (Cambridge, MA: Harvard University Press, 2012), pp. 58–64.

12. See, for example, Gavin Wright, "The Origins of American Industrial Success, 1879–1940," *American Economic Review* 80:4 (September 1990), 651–68; Alfred D.

Chandler Jr., *The Visible Hand: The Managerial Revolution in American Business* (Cambridge, MA: Harvard University Press, 1977); Jack High, "Economic Theory and the Rise of Big Business in America, 1870–1910," *Business History Review* 85 (Spring 2011), 85–112.

13. See, for example, Richard Franklin Bensel, *The Political Economy of American Industrialization, 1877–1900* (New York: Cambridge University Press, 2000), pp. 4–11, 518–20.

14. Bensel, *Political Economy*, pp. 321–49, Howard Gillman, "How Political Parties Can Use the Courts to Advance Their Agendas: Federal Courts in the United States, 1875–1891," *American Political Science Review* 96:3 (September 2002), 511–24.

15. On the gold standard and the crises: Hugh Rockoff, "Banking and Finance, 1789–1914," ch. 14 in Engerman and Gallman (eds.), *Cambridge Economic History of the United States*, vol. 2, *The Long Nineteenth Century*; Bensel, *Political Economy*, pp. 366–73.

16. Bensel, *Political Economy*, p. 371.

17. Rockoff, "Banking and Finance," p. 663; Bensel, *Political Economy*, pp. 366–73, quotation at p. 371. On the logic and practice of distributive politics: Theodore J. Lowi, "American Business, Public Policy, Case-Studies, and Political Theory," *World Politics* 16:4 (1964), 677–715.

18. Bensel, *Political Economy*, p. 371.

19. On the politics of the late nineteenth-century tariff: Bensel, *Political Economy*, ch. 7.

20. E. E. Schattschneider, *Politics, Pressures, and the Tariff: A Study of Free Private Enterprise in Pressure Politics, as Shown in the 1929–1930 Revision of the Tariff* (New York: Prentice-Hall, 1935), pp. 283–84. This book centers on the Smoot-Hawley tariff of 1930, but its logic extends back in time, as its author surely knew.

21. See for example Robert C. Allen, "American Exceptionalism as a Problem in Global History," *Journal of Economic History* 74:2 (June 2014), 309–350, at 339; James MacDonald, *When Globalization Fails: The Rise and Fall of Pax Americana* (New York: Farrar Straus and Giroux, 2015), pp. 28–30.

22. On the revenue reliance: John Mark Hansen, "Taxation and the Political Economy of the Tariff," *International Organization* 44:4 (Autumn 1990), 527–51. On the Republicans' general principle of neo-mercantilism: John Gerring, *Party Ideologies in America, 1828–1896* (New York: Cambridge University Press, 1998), pp. 64–78; Charles W. Calhoun, "Political Economy in the Gilded Age: The Republican Party's Industrial Policy," *Journal of Policy History* 8:3 (1996), 291–309, pp. 294–99. See also S.

Walter Poulshock, "Pennsylvania and the Politics of the Tariff, 1880–1888," *Pennsylvania History* 29:3 (July 1962), 291–305.

23. Robert E. Lipsey, "U.S. Foreign Trade and the Balance of Payments, 1800–1913," ch. 15 in Engerman and Gallman (eds.), *Cambridge Economic History of the United States,* vol. 2, *The Long Nineteenth Century,* p. 727; Stanley L. Engerman and Kenneth L. Sokoloff, "Technology and Industrialization, 1790–1914," ch. 9 in Engerman and Gallman (eds.), *Cambridge Economic History of the United States,* vol. 2, *The Long Nineteenth Century,* pp. 398–401.

24. Gregory J. Wawro and Eric Schickler, *Filibuster: Obstruction and Lawmaking in the U.S. Senate* (Princeton, NJ: Princeton University Press, 2006), ch. 6.

25. On Congress dominating the process: Lawrence H. Chamberlain, *The President, Congress and Legislation* (New York: Columbia University Press, 1946), ch. 3.

26. See David Karol, "Congress, the President, and Elite Opinion in Historical Perspective," paper presented at Congress and History Conference, Columbia University, New York, June 21–22, 2013, pp. 27–31. Accounts of the White House's distinctive free-trade bent, at least during recent times, appear in William R. Keech and Kyoungsan Pak, "Partisanship, Institutions, and Change in American Trade Politics," *Journal of Politics* 57:4 (1995), 1130–42, at 1136–40; Orin Kirshner, "Superpower Politics: The Triumph of Free Trade in Postwar America," *Critical Review* 19:4 (2007), 523–42.

27. Calhoun makes this case in "Political Economy in the Gilded Age," quotation at 292.

28. Daniel Walker Howe, *The Political Culture of the American Whigs* (Chicago: University of Chicago Press, 1984), ch. 6; Merrill D. Peterson, *The Great Triumvirate: Webster, Clay, and Calhoun* (New York: Oxford University Press, 1987); J. Joseph Huthmacher, *Senator Robert F. Wagner and the Rise of Urban Liberalism* (New York: Atheneum, 1968). On the prominence of Sherman as a congressional actor, see David R. Mayhew, *America's Congress: Actions in the Public Sphere, James Madison through Newt Gingrich* (New Haven, CT: Yale University Press, 2000), pp. 62–64, 168–71.

29. Sherman's take on these matters can be found in his *Recollections of Forty Years in the House, Senate and Cabinet: An Autobiography,* vols. 1 and 2 (Chicago: Werner Company, 1895). He hops around. The best nuggets are in vol. 1, chs. 11–13, 15, 17, 20, 22, 24–26; vol. 2, chs. 32, 36, 57, 63, 64. On Sherman's role in the 1860s and 1870s, see also Sharkey, *Money, Class, and Party,* passim.

30. Milton Friedman argues that denying an alternative silver standard in the much-assailed Coinage Act of 1873 may have been a policy mistake—too much

deflation ensued. See "The Crime of 1873," *Journal of Political Economy* 98:6 (December 1990), 1159–94. Friedman sees a mistake in this decision, not, as others once alleged, a crime. The pro-gold forces of the late nineteenth century were "sincere believers that the gold standard was the only satisfactory pillar for a financially stable society" (1178).

31. Wyatt Wells, "Rhetoric of the Standards: The Debate over Gold and Silver in the 1890s," *Journal of the Gilded Age and Progressive Era* 14 (2015), 49–68, at 56–59.

32. Wells, "Rhetoric of the Standards," 59.

33. Quotation from Prasad, *Land of Too Much,* p. xii.

34. On the size of the firms: Prasad, *Land of Too Much,* pp. 75–76.

35. On European socialism: E. J. Hobsbawm, *Age of Empire, 1875–1914* (New York: Pantheon, 1987), ch. 5. For a comparison that emphasizes contrast, see Melvyn Stokes, "American Progressives and the European Left," *Journal of American Studies* 17:1 (April 1983), 5–28.

36. William L. Letwin, "Congress and the Sherman Antitrust Law: 1887–1890," *University of Chicago Law Review* 23:2 (Winter 1956), 221–58, quotation at 226. See also Prasad, *Land of Too Much,* pp. 188–90.

37. The story is told in Prasad, *Land of Too Much,* pp. 74–76, 89–90, 103–09; Elizabeth Sanders, *Roots of Reform: Farmers, Workers, and the American State, 1877–1917* (Chicago: University of Chicago Press, 1999), chs. 6–8; Ronald L. Feinman, *Twilight of Progressivism: The Western Republican Senators and the New Deal* (Baltimore: Johns Hopkins University Press, 1981), ch. 1; David A. Horowitz, *Beyond Left and Right: Insurgency and the Establishment* (Urbana: University of Illinois Press, 1997), chs. 1, 3. Horowitz carries the story through the 1920s.

38. See Peter J. Coleman, "New Zealand Liberalism and the Origins of the American Welfare State," *Journal of American History* 69 (1982), 372–91.

39. Horowitz, *Beyond Left and Right,* pp. 5–6.

40. Rounded discussions of the politics of railroad regulation, the pioneer cause of the time, appear in Stephen Skowronek, *Building a New American State: The Expansion of National Administrative Capacities, 1877–1920* (New York: Cambridge University Press, 1982), ch. 5; Robert Dawson Kennedy Jr., "The Statist Evolution of Rail Governance in the United States, 1830–1986," ch. 5 in John L. Campbell, J. Rogers Hollingsworth, and Leon N. Lindberg (eds.), *Governance of the American Economy* (New York: Cambridge University Press, 1991), at pp. 154–64; Robert E. Gallamore and John R. Meyer, *American Railroads: Decline and Renaissance in the Twentieth Century* (Cambridge, MA: Harvard University Press, 2014), ch. 2.

41. Prasad, *Land of Too Much,* p. 184.

42. William H. Becker, "Managerial Capitalism and Public Policy," *Business and Economic History* 21 (1992), 247–56, quotation at 248.

43. See Kimberly J. Morgan and Monica Prasad, "The Origins of Tax Systems: A French-American Comparison," *American Journal of Sociology* 114:5 (March 2009), 1350–94; Prasad, *Land of Too Much,* pp. 16–18, Sven Steinmo, *Taxation and Democracy: Swedish, British, and American Approaches to Financing the Modern State* (New Haven, CT: Yale University Press, 1993), ch. 2.

44. Quoted in Annie Lowrey, "For Two Economists, the Buffett Rule Is Just a Start," *New York Times,* online, April 16, 2012, available at www.nytimes.com/2012/04/17/business/for-economists-saez-and-piketty-the-buffett-rule-is-just-a-start.html.

45. The contrast is drawn in Michael McGerr, "Progressivism, Liberalism, and the Rich," paper presented at conference on "The Progressives' Century: Democratic Reform and Constitutional Government in the United States," Representation and Governance," Yale University, New Haven, Connecticut, November 1–2, 2013.

46. Joseph J. Thorndike, " 'The Unfair Advantage of the Few': The New Deal Origins of 'Soak the Rich' Taxation," ch. 2 in Isaac William Martin, Ajay K. Mehrotra, and Monica Prasad (eds.), *The New Fiscal Sociology: Taxation in Comparative Historical Perspective* (New York: Cambridge University Press, 2009).

47. On the record in business regulation in general, see Prasad, *Land of Too Much,* ch. 7; Sanders, *Roots of Reform,* ch. 6. On railroad regulation, see Chamberlain, *President, Congress, and Legislation,* ch. 11.

48. Chamberlain, *President, Congress, and Legislation,* p. 414. Cleveland just signed the bill.

49. Sanders, *Roots of Reform,* p. 272. See also Chamberlain, *President, Congress, and Legislation,* pp. 30–32. On the subsequent evolution, see for example Naomi Lamoreaux, *The Great Merger Movement in American Business, 1895–1904* (New York: Cambridge University Press, 1988); Becker, "Managerial Capitalism and Public Policy."

50. Sanders, *Roots of Reform,* p. 208.

51. On the Hepburn Act: Sanders, *Roots of Reform,* pp. 198–202; Jeffrey K. Tulis, *The Rhetorical Presidency* (Princeton, NJ: Princeton University Press, 1987), ch. 4. On the Pure Food and Drugs Act: James Harvey Young, *Pure Food: Securing the Federal Food and Drugs Act of 1906* (Princeton, NJ: Princeton University Press, 1989), chs. 1, 3, 7–11.

52. Gyung-Ho Jeong, Gary J. Miller, and Andrew C. Sobel, "Political Compromise and Bureaucratic Structure: The Political Origins of the Federal Reserve System," *Journal of Law, Economics, and Organization* 25:2 (2008), 472–98, quotations at 473, 479. For a detailed account of the assembling of the enactment, see Roger Lowenstein, *America's Bank: The Epic Struggle to Create the Federal Reserve* (New York: Penguin, 2015), chs. 12, 13.

53. William G. Whittaker, "The Davis-Bacon Act: Institutional Evolution and Public Policy," available at http://congressionalresearch.com/94-408/document.php?study=The+Davis-Bacon+Act+Institutional+Evolution+and+Public+Policy (November 30, 2007).

54. On the Norris–La Guardia Act: Christopher L. Tomlins, "Labor Law," ch. 11 in Stanley L. Engerman and Robert E. Gallman (eds.), *The Cambridge Economic History of the United States*, vol. 3, *The Twentieth Century* (New York: Cambridge University Press, 2000), pp. 669–70.

55. Huthmacher, *Senator Robert F. Wagner*, pp. 146–48, 158–71, 189–98; Chamberlain, *President, Congress, and Legislation*, ch. 4. See also Tomlins, "Labor Law," pp. 670–75; Theda Skocpol, Kenneth Finegold, and Michael Goldfield, "Explaining New Deal Labor Policy," *American Political Science Review* 84:4 (December 1990), 1297–1315, at 1298–1300; Dennis W. Johnson, *The Laws That Shaped America: Fifteen Acts and Their Lasting Impact* (New York: Routledge, 2009), p. 142.

56. Huthmacher, *Senator Robert F. Wagner*, p. 197.

57. Huthmacher, *Senator Robert F. Wagner*, pp. 163, 166, 190, 195–98.

58. On the record in progressive taxation in general: Prasad, *Land of Too Much*, pp. 125–29; Steinmo, *Taxation and Democracy*, pp. 68–79; David E. Kyvig, *Explicit and Authentic Acts: Amending the U. S. Constitution, 1776–1995* (Lawrence: University Press of Kansas, 1996), pp. 201–04. On Bryan: David D. Anderson, *William Jennings Bryan* (Boston: Twayne, 1981), pp. 65–67; Paul W. Glad, *The Trumpet Soundeth: William Jennings Bryan and His Democracy, 1896–1912* (Lincoln: University of Nebraska Press, 1960), p. 86. On President Cleveland: Steinmo, *Taxation and Democracy*, p. 71; John F. Witte, *The Politics and Development of the Federal Income Tax* (Madison: University of Wisconsin Press, 1985), p. 71.

59. Steinmo, *Taxation and Democracy*, pp. 74–76; John D. Buenker, *The Income Tax and the Progressive Era* (New York: Garland, 1985), ch. 2. Final state ratification of the amendment followed in 1913.

60. Witte, *Politics and Development of the Federal Income Tax*, pp. 75–79; Buenker, *Income Tax*, ch. 8.

61. Buenker, *Income Tax*, p. 338.

62. W. Elliot Brownlee, "Tax Regimes, National Crises, and State-Building in America," ch. 2 in Brownlee (ed.), *Funding the Modern American State, 1941–1995: The Rise and Fall of the Era of Easy Finance* (New York: Cambridge University Press, 1996), pp. 60–66; W. Elliot Brownlee, "Wilson and Financing the Modern State: The Revenue Act of 1916," *Proceedings of the American Philosophical Society* 129:2 (June 1985), 173–210, quotation at 177; Sanders, *Roots of Reform*, p. 230.

63. That juncture's surge in inheritance taxation can be seen in Kenneth Scheve and David Stasavage, "Democracy, War, and Wealth: Lessons from Two Centuries of Inheritance Taxation," *American Political Science Review* 106:1 (February 2012), 81–102, at 86, 89.

64. Brownlee, "Tax Regimes, National Crises, and State-Building in America," p. 61.

65. Brownlee, "Tax Regimes, National Crises, and State-Building in America," pp. 68–70.

66. W. Elliot Brownlee, *Federal Taxation in America: A Short History*, 2nd ed. (New York: Cambridge University Press, 2004), pp. 83–84.

67. For comment on the political value of such a presentation, see David R. Mayhew, "Legislation," ch. 5 in Leon Lipson and Stanton Wheeler (eds.), *Law and the Social Sciences* (New York: Russell Sage Foundation, 1986), pp. 276–77.

68. An earlier instance is 1812 vis-à-vis Britain. James L. Sundquist highlights the 1812 and 1898 instances in *The Decline and Resurgence of Congress* (Washington, DC: Brookings Press, 1981), p. 94.

69. Fareed Zakaria, *From Wealth to Power: The Unusual Origins of America's World Role* (Princeton, NJ: Princeton University Press, 1998), ch. 3; Colin D. Moore, "State Building through Partnership: Delegation, Public-Private Partnerships, and the Political Development of American Imperialism, 1898–1916," *Studies in American Political Development* 25 (April 2011), 27–55; John J. Tierney Jr., *Chasing Ghosts: Unconventional Warfare in American History* (Washington, DC: Potomac Books, 2006), chs. 10–12; Horowitz, *Beyond Left and Right*, pp. 40–42; Nugent, *Habits of Empire*, pp. 256–63, 276.

70. Jeffrey W. Meiser, *Power and Restraint: The Rise of the United States, 1898–1941* (Washington, D.C.: Georgetown University Press, 2015).

71. On Versailles: William C. Widenor, *Henry Cabot Lodge and the Search for an American Foreign Policy* (Berkeley: University of California Press, 1980). On the World Court: Horowitz, *Beyond Left and Right*, pp. 163–64.

72. Wayne S. Cole, *Senator Gerald P. Nye and American Foreign Relations* (Minneapolis: University of Minnesota Press, 1962), quotation at 73; Horowitz, *Beyond Left and Right,* ch. 8; Feinman, *Twilight of Progressivism,* ch. 9; Lynne Olson, *Those Angry Days: Roosevelt, Lindbergh, and America's Fight over World War II, 1939–1941* (New York: Random House, 2013), chs. 4, 18, 22, 23.

73. See Mark Kesselman, "Presidential Leadership in Congress on Foreign Policy: A Replication of a Hypothesis," *Midwest Journal of Political Science* 9:4 (March 1965), 401–06.

74. On Indochina: Thomas M. Franck and Edward Weisband, *Foreign Policy by Congress* (New York: Oxford University Press, 1979), ch. 1.

75. Zakaria, *From Wealth to Power,* p. 88.

76. Douglas Kriner, "Accountability without Deliberation: Separation of Powers in Times of War," *Boston University Law Review* 92 (2015), 1275–96, at 1286. On members being attuned to the later "traceability" of their position taking, see R. Douglas Arnold, *The Logic of Congressional Action* (New Haven, CT: Yale University Press, 1990).

77. Thomas B. Pepinsky, "Trade Competition and American Decolonization," *World Politics* 67:3 (July 2015), 387–422, quotation at 387.

78. Theodore Friend, *Between Two Empires: The Ordeal of the Philippines, 1929–1946* (New Haven, CT: Yale University Press, 1965), chs. 7, 8, 11; H. W. Brands, *Bound to Empire: The United States and the Philippines* (New York: Oxford University Press, 1992), pp. 149–57.

79. Hobsbawm notes the relative sparseness of U.S. colonies in *Age of Empire,* pp. 58, 67.

80. For an exceptionally well-argued case for presidency-Congress relations as a cause, see Meiser, *Power and Restraint.* On the geostrategy, see for example David Milne, *Worldmaking: The Art and Science of American Diplomacy* (New York: Farrar Straus and Giroux, 2015), ch. 1.

81. For a discussion of the United States in this regard, see Stephen D. Krasner, *Defending the National Interest: Raw Materials Investments and U.S. Foreign Policy* (Princeton, NJ: Princeton University Press, 1978), ch. 1.

82. Robert A. Dahl, *Congress and Foreign Policy* (New York: Harcourt, Brace, 1950), p. 3.

83. For a textured discussion of Congress's role during the interwar era, see David A. Lake, *Entangling Relations: American Foreign Policy in Its Century* (Princeton, NJ: Princeton University Press, 1999), ch. 4.

84. On Congress's historical role in foreign policy, especially its exercises of opposition: Mayhew, *America's Congress*, pp. 103–22.

85. Arthur M. Schlesinger Jr., *The Imperial Presidency* (Boston: Houghton Mifflin, 1973).

86. John Chettle, "The American Way: Or How the Chaos, Unpredictability, Contradictions, Complexity, and Example of Our System Undid Communism and Apartheid," *The National Interest* 41 (Fall 1995), 3–18.

87. On the role of hegemon, see for Nuno P. Monteiro, *Theory of Unipolar Politics* (New York: Cambridge University Press, 2014). On the liberal capitalist order, see Robert Kagan, *The World America Made* (New York: Vintage Books, 2013).

Chapter 4. Depression and the Welfare State

1. Ira Katznelson, *Fear Itself: The New Deal and the Origins of Our Time* (New York: Liveright Publishing, 2013), p. 20.

2. See, for example, Peter Gourevitch, "Breaking with Orthodoxy: The Politics of Economic Policy Responses to the Depression of the 1930s," *International Organization* 38:1 (Winter 1984), 95–129; Ekkart Zimmermann and Thomas Saalfeld, "Economic and Political Reactions to the World Economic Crisis of the 1930s in Six European Countries," *International Studies Quarterly* 32:3 (September 1988), 305–34.

3. The least familiar of these responses, perhaps, is Japan's abandonment of liberal politics in reaction to the collapse of the country's economy in 1929–32. A deft recent account appears in Harukata Takenaka, *Failed Democratization in Prewar Japan: Breakdown of a Hybrid Regime* (Stanford, CA: Stanford University Press, 2014), ch. 6.

4. Katznelson, *Fear Itself*, pt. I.

5. Randall E. Parker (ed.), *The Economics of the Great Depression: A Twenty-First Century Look Back at the Economics of the Interwar Era* (Northampton, MA: Edward Elgar, 2007), pp. 25–28 (first quotation by Parker at 26), 45 (second quotation by Peter Temin at 45), 53–54 and 66 (comments by Ben Bernanke), 154 (comment by Barry Eichengreen); Michael D. Bordo, Claudia Goldin, and Eugene N. White, "The Defining Moment Hypothesis: The Editors' Introduction," pp. 1–10 in *The Defining Moment: The Great Depression and the American Economy in the Twentieth Century* (Chicago: University of Chicago Press, 1998), at p. 10; Charles W. Calomiris and David C. Wheelock, "Was the Great Depression a Watershed for American Monetary Policy?" ch. 1 in Bordo, Goldin, and White (eds.), *Defining Moment*, pp. 27–32; Christina D. Romer, "What Ended the Great Depression?" *Journal of Economic History* 52:4 (December 1992), 757–84, at 759, 773, 781. For this judgment

about going off gold, see also Kim Quaile Hill, *Democracies in Crisis: Public Policy Responses to the Great Depression* (Boulder, CO: Westview Press, 1988), p. 69. On FDR's monetary moves, see also Liaquat Ahamed, *Lords of Finance: The Bankers Who Broke the World* (New York: Penguin, 2009), ch. 1.

6. See Parker (ed.), *Economics of the Great Depression*, pp. 18–21.

7. For this familiar package, see for example Alonzo L. Hamby, *For the Survival of Democracy: Franklin Roosevelt and the World Crisis of the 1930s* (New York: Free Press, 2004), ch. 4; Anthony J. Badger, *FDR: The First Hundred Days* (New York: Hill and Wang, 2008); Parker (ed.), *Economics of the Great Depression*, pp. 25–28; Calomiris and Wheelock, "Was the Great Depression a Watershed for American Monetary Policy?," in Bordo, Goldin, and White (eds.), *Defining Moment*, pp. 27–32; David M. Kennedy, *Freedom from Fear: The American People in Depression and War, 1929–1945* (New York: Oxford University Press, 1999), ch. 5.

8. Hamby, *For the Survival of Democracy*, p. 126.

9. Wilfred E. Binkley, *President and Congress*, 3rd ed. (New York: Vintage Books, 1962), p. 307. See also Christine M. Bradley, "A Historical Perspective on Deposit Insurance Coverage," *FDIC Banking Review* 13:2, pp. 1–25, at pp. 5–7, available at www.fdic.gov/bank/analytical/banking/2000dec/brv13n2_1.pdf.

10. Edwin Amenta, *Bold Relief: Institutional Politics and the Origins of Modern American Social Policy* (Princeton, NJ: Princeton University Press, 1998); Hamby, *For the Survival of Democracy*, pp. 275–76.

11. Amenta, *Bold Relief*, pp. 4–7, 76–77, quotations at pp. 7, 4–5.

12. Parker, *Economics of the Great Depression*, 25, 27–28 (comments by Parker); 54–55, 66 (comments by Ben Bernanke), 90–91, 100 (comments by Robert Lucas), 105–06 (comment by Lee Ohanian), 125 (comment by Christina Romer). See also Hamby, *For the Survival of Democracy*, pp. 164–74, 418; Kennedy, *Freedom from Fear*, pp. 177–89. A recent interpretation more favorable to the NIRA is Gauti B. Eggertsson, "Was the New Deal Contractionary?" *American Economic Review* 102:1 (2012), 524–55.

13. See for example Kenneth Finegold and Theda Skocpol, *State and Party in America's New Deal* (Madison: University of Wisconsin Press, 1995), ch. 3; Lawrence H. Chamberlain, *The President, Congress and Legislation* (New York: Columbia University Press, 1946), p. 58.

14. See Jordan A. Schwarz, "John Nance Garner and the Sales Tax Rebellion of 1932," *Journal of Southern History* 30:2 (May 1964), 162–80; W. Elliot Brownlee, *Federal Taxation in America: A Short History*, 2nd ed. (New York: Cambridge University Press, 2004), pp. 83–84.

15. The subject is complicated. See Ellen R. McGrattan, "Capital Taxation During the U.S. Great Depression," *Quarterly Journal of Economics* 127:3 (2012), 1515–50; Hamby, *For the Survival of Democracy,* pp. 300–03, 312–13; Mark Leff, *The Limits of Symbolic Reform: The New Deal and Taxation, 1933–1939* (New York: Cambridge University Press, 1984), chs. 3, 4; W. Elliot Brownlee, "Tax Regimes, National Crises, and State-Building in America," ch. 2 in Brownlee (ed.), *Funding the Modern American State, 1941–1995: The Rise and Fall of the Era of Easy Finance* (New York: Cambridge University Press, 1996), pp. 76–81; Joseph J. Thorndike, " 'The Unfair Advantage of the Few': The New Deal Origins of 'Soak the Rich' Taxation," ch. 2 in Isaac William Martin, Ajay K. Mehrotra, and Monica Prasad (eds.), *The New Fiscal Sociology: Taxation in Comparative Historical Perspective* (New York: Cambridge University Press, 2009).

16. See for example the brief comment by James Hamilton in Parker (ed.), *Economics of the Great Depression,* p. 80, and the interpretation in Hamby, *For the Survival of Democracy,* pp. 90, 284–86, 300–03, 313–14, 356–58. On antitrust, see Alan Brinkley, *The End of Reform: New Deal Liberalism in Recession and War* (New York: Alfred A. Knopf, 1995), ch. 6.

17. Hill, *Democracies in Crisis,* p. 57.

18. Romer, "What Ended the Great Depression?" p. 781.

19. A summary view in Parker (ed.), *Economics of the Great Depression,* p. 26.

20. Hill, *Democracies in Crisis,* chs. 4, 5. Recovery patterns in a dozen or so democracies are examined in this study. Across them, variation in monetary policies (involving gold, etc.) seems to have dominated variation in compensatory fiscal policies as an explanation of recovery. Going off the gold standard early rather than late seems to have helped a great deal (p. 69). To cite some thought-provoking instances, a "classical" regimen of balanced budgets and free-market policies went hand in hand with relatively quick recoveries in Australia, Britain, Finland, and Norway. Yes, it is true that those particular countries had suffered relatively modest downtowns, yet it is additionally true that their modest downturns corresponded to going off gold early (pp. 50–58). It is a complicated matter. Yet the author sees his findings as "in striking contradiction to the widely held popular conception that stimulus fiscal policy was the most successful governmental tool for recovery in the depression" (pp. 39–40).

21. Hamby, *For the Survival of Democracy,* pp. 64–75, chs. 4, 5, 7.

22. The Keynes story is reported in Alonzo L. Hamby, *Man of Destiny: FDR and the Making of the American Century* (New York: Basic Books, 2015), pp. 269–72; Kennedy, *Freedom from Fear,* pp. 357–58.

23. Hamby, *For the Survival of Democracy,* p. 418.

24. Comments by Christina Romer and James Butkiewicz in Parker (ed.), *Economics of the Great Depression,* pp. 131, 184–85.

25. Badger, *FDR,* pp. 72–73.

26. Binkley, *President and Congress,* p. 308.

27. E. Cary Brown, "Fiscal Policy in the Thirties: A Reappraisal," *American Economic Review* 46:5 (1956), 857–79.

28. A new, comprehensive account is Stephen R. Ortiz, *Beyond the Bonus March and GI Bill: How Veteran Politics Shaped the New Deal Era* (New York: NYU Press, 2010). On the politics of the bonus in the 1920s and 1930s: V. O. Key Jr., "The Veterans and the House of Representatives: A Study of a Pressure Group and Electoral Mortality," *Journal of Politics* 5:1 (1943), 27–40.

29. Ortiz, *Beyond the Bonus March,* p. 39, ch. 6 (see also p. 96 regarding a 1934 veto override); Brown, "Fiscal Policy in the Thirties"; Lester G. Telser, "The Veterans' Bonus of 1936," *Journal of Post Keynesian Economics* 26:2 (2003), 227–44.

30. Ortiz, *Beyond the Bonus March,* p. 176.

31. Telser, "Veterans' Bonus," abstract.

32. Joshua K. Hausman, "Fiscal Policy and Economic Recovery: The Case of the 1936 Veterans' Bonus," *American Economic Review* 106:4 (2016), 1101–1143.

33. On variously the lateness and leanness: Peter H. Lindert, "The Rise of Social Spending, 1880–1930," *Explorations in Economic History* 31 (1994), 1–37, at 1; Jacob S. Hacker, *The Divided Welfare State: The Battle over Public and Private Social Benefits in the United States* (New York: Cambridge University Press, 2002), p. 7; Martha Derthick, *Policymaking for Social Security* (Washington, DC: Brookings, 1979), p. 10; Ann Shola Orloff and Theda Skocpol, "Why Not Equal Protection? Explaining the Politics of Public Social Spending in Britain, 1900–1911, and the United States, 1880–1920," ch. V.2 in David Englander (ed.), *Britain and America: Studies in Comparative History, 1760–1970* (New Haven, CT: Yale University Press, 1997), p. 242; Mark Stabile and Sarah Thompson, "The Changing Role of Government in Financing Health Care: An International Perspective," *Journal of Economic Literature* 52:2 (2014), 480–518, at 481.

34. See Stephen Skowronek, *Building a New American State: The Expansion of National Administrative Capacities, 1877–1920* (New York: Cambridge University Press, 1982), ch. 3, at especially pp. 56–59, 64–67, 69, 73, 74, 78 (an exception to the generalization), 80–81, quotation at 81.

35. Orloff and Skocpol, "Why Not Equal Protection?" pp. 266–69, quotation at 268; more generally, Theda Skocpol, *Protecting Soldiers and Mothers: The Political*

Origins of Social Policy in the United States (Cambridge, MA: Harvard University Press, 1992), chs. 1, 5.

36. Skocpol, *Protecting Soldiers and Mothers,* ch. 2.

37. David R. Mayhew, *Congress: The Electoral Connection* (New Haven, CT: Yale University Press, 1974).

38. Charles Francis Adams, "The Civil-War Pension Lack-of-System: A Four-Thousand-Million Record of Legislative Incompetence Leading to General Political Corruption," dated 1912, reprinted from *The World's Work.* On the interest group ingredient, see Scott Ainsworth, "Electoral Strength and the Emergence of Group Influence in the late 1800s: The Grand Army of the Republic," *American Politics Quarterly* 23:3 (July 1995), 319–38; Scott Ainsworth, "Lobbyists as Interest Group Entrepreneurs: The Mobilization of Union Veterans," *American Review of Politics* 16 (Summer 1995), 107–29.

39. Orloff and Skocpol, "Why Not Equal Protection?" p. 267.

40. Monica Prasad, *The Land of Too Much: American Abundance and the Paradox of Poverty* (Cambridge, MA: Harvard University Press, 2012), pp. xi–xiv, 122–24, 147–53, 170–71.

41. G. John Ikenberry and Theda Skocpol, "Expanding Social Benefits: The Role of Social Security," *Political Science Quarterly* 102:3 (Autumn 1987), 389–416, at 405.

42. For an account of the enactment process, see James MacGregor Burns, *Congress on Trial: The Legislative Process and the Administrative State* (New York: Harper and Brothers, 1949), pp. 68–82.

43. The drives by the postwar presidents through 2000 are covered in David Blumenthal and James A. Morone, *The Heart of Power: Health and Politics in the Oval Office* (Berkeley: University of California Press, 2010). On Medicare, Blumenthal and Morone are in the Johnson corner; an account on the Mills side is Julian E. Zelizer, *Taxing America: Wilbur D. Mills, Congress, and the State, 1945–1975* (New York: Cambridge University Press, 1998), ch. 7. Standard accounts of Medicare include Theodore R. Marmor, *The Politics of Medicare* (Chicago: Aldine, 1973).

44. Blumenthal and Morone, *Heart of Power,* ch. 3.

45. Derthick, *Policymaking for Social Security,* p. 38.

46. On 1939: Hacker, *Divided Welfare State,* pp. 108–12. On 1968–72: Hacker, *Divided Welfare State,* pp. 142–45; Derthick, *Policymaking for Social Security,* ch. 17.

47. Charles Homans, "Marathon Man," *Washington Monthly,* May-June 2009. See also Shanna Rose, *Financing Medicaid: Federalism and the Growth of America's*

Health Care Safety Net (Ann Arbor: University of Michigan Press, 2013), pp. 20, 110–13, 117–19, 123–28, 133.

48. On 1912 and 1921: Skocpol, *Protecting Soldiers and Mothers*, ch. 9. On disability benefits: Derthick, *Policymaking for Social Security*, ch. 15. On SSI: Edward D. Berkowitz and Larry DeWitt, *The Other Welfare: Supplemental Security Income and U.S. Social Policy* (Ithaca, NY: Cornell University Press, 2013), ch. 1. On EITC: Christopher Howard, *The Hidden Welfare State: Tax Expenditures and Social Policy in the United States* (Princeton, NJ: Princeton University Press, 1997), ch. 3.

49. J. Joseph Huthmacher, *Senator Robert F. Wagner and the Rise of Urban Liberalism* (New York: Atheneum, 1968), pp. 224–28; Binkley, *President and Congress*, p. 307.

50. On 1944: Nancy Beck Young, *Why We Fight: Congress and the Politics of World War II* (Lawrence: University Press of Kansas, 2013), pp. 226–29. On 1984 and 2008: "GI Bill Education Benefits Expanded," *Congressional Quarterly Almanac 2008* online, available at http://library.cqpress.com/cqalmanac/document-php?id=c qal08-1090-52025-2174861.

51. Hacker, *Divided Welfare State*, pp. 115–21, 238–43; Prasad, *Land of Too Much*, pp. 153–59; Howard, *Hidden Welfare State*, pp. 115–21.

52. Hacker, *Divided Welfare State*, pp. 163–72, 238–43; Howard, *Hidden Welfare State*, ch. 6; James A. Wooten, *The Employee Retirement Income Security Act of 1974: A Political History* (Berkeley: University of California Press, 2004).

53. Kimberly J. Morgan and Andrea Louise Campbell, *The Delegated Welfare State: Medicare, Markets, and the Governance of Social Policy* (New York: Oxford University Press, 2011), pp. 7–8, 35, 46–47.

Chapter 5. After World War II

The "Postwar Prosperity" section borrows heavily from David R. Mayhew, "The Long 1950s as a Policy Era," ch. 2 in Jeffery A. Jenkins and Sidney M. Milkis (eds.), *The Politics of Major Policy Reform in Postwar America* (New York: Cambridge University Press, 2014), available at http://campuspress.yale.edu/davidmayhew/.

1. Charles S. Maier, "The Politics of Productivity: Foundations of American Economic Policy after World War II," *International Organization* 31:4 (Autumn 1977), 607–33, quotation at 609.

2. M. Stephen Weatherford and Lorraine M. McDonnell, "Macroeconomic Policy Making beyond the Electoral Construct," pp. 95–113 in George C. Edwards III, Steven A. Shull, and Norman C. Thomas (eds.), *The Presidency and Public Policy Making* (Pittsburgh, PA: University of Pittsburgh Press, 1985).

3. Allen J. Matusow, *The Unraveling of America: A History of Liberalism in the 1960s* (New York: Harper & Row, 1984), p. xix.

4. M. M. Postan, *An Economic History of Western Europe, 1945–1964* (London: Methuen, 1967), p. 25. See also Mark Mazower, *Dark Continent: Europe's Twentieth Century* (New York: Alfred A. Knopf, 1999), pp. 292–98.

5. Tony Judt, *Postwar: A History of Europe Since 1945* (New York: Penguin, 2005), p. 324.

6. Eric Hobsbawm, *The Age of Extremes: A History of the World, 1914–1991* (New York: Pantheon, 1994), ch. 9, pp. 257–59, quotation at pp. 257–58.

7. Alan Brinkley, *The End of Reform: New Liberalism in Recession and War* (New York: Alfred A. Knopf, 1995), pp. 245–64; Ira Katznelson, *Fear Itself: The New Deal and the Origins of Our Time* (New York: Liveright, 2013), pp. 373–81; John W. Jeffries, "The 'New' New Deal: FDR and American Liberalism, 1937–1945," *Political Science Quarterly* 105:3 (Autumn 1990), 397–418; Edwin Amenta, *Bold Relief: Institutional Politics and the Origins of Modern American Social Policy* (Princeton, NJ: Princeton University Press, 1998), pp. 191–92, 199–202. On the enactment of the Employment Act of 1946, see Stephen Kemp Bailey's classic study *Congress Makes a Law: The Story Behind the Employment Act of 1946* (New York: Columbia University Press, 1950); Robert M. Collins, *The Business Response to Keynes, 1929–1964* (New York: Columbia University Press, 1981), pp. 99–109.

8. Benn Steil, *The Battle of Bretton Woods: John Maynard Keynes, Harry Dexter White, and the Making of a New World Order* (Princeton, NJ: Princeton University Press, 2013). The slight role of Congress and its members appears at pp. 206–07, 211, 213, 222, 245, 255–60.

9. W. Elliot Brownlee, "The Public Sector," in Stanley L. Engerman and Robert E. Gallman (eds.), *The Cambridge Economic History of the United States,* vol. 3, *The Twentieth Century* (New York: Cambridge University Press, 2000), p. 1050. The war case has been made for Britain, also: "The key to the institutionalization of the new paradigm was the shock of war—the decisive factor in forcing the Treasury radically to reappraise its ideas on economic policy." Michael J. Oliver and Hugh Pemberton, "Learning and Change in 20th-Century British Economic Policy," *Governance* 17:3 (July 2004), 415–41, quotation at 423–24.

10. See Bailey, *Congress Makes a Law.* On the executive location of post-1946 economic management, see for example Herbert Stein, *Presidential Economics: The Making of Economic Policy from Roosevelt to Reagan and Beyond* (New York: Simon and Schuster, 1984), ch. 3.

11. Dwight D. Eisenhower, *The White House Years: Mandate for Change, 1953–1956* (Garden City, NY: Doubleday, 1963), p. 388, second quotation in note 10.

12. Eisenhower, *The White House Years: Mandate for Change,* p. 548.

13. Eisenhower, *The White House Years: Mandate for Change,* p. 389.

14. The growth aim of this tax cut is brought out in Herbert S. Parmet, *JFK: The Presidency of John F. Kennedy* (New York: Dial Press, 1983), p. 94; Theodore C. Sorensen, *Kennedy* (New York: Harper and Row, 1965), pp. 429–30; Matusow, *Unraveling of America,* pp. 49–59.

15. James L. Sundquist, *Politics and Policy: The Eisenhower, Kennedy, and Johnson Years* (Washington, DC: Brookings, 1968).

16. See Mayhew, "Long 1950s as a Policy Era," p. 37.

17. Interesting recent work on some of these enactments includes Edward L. Schapsmeier and Frederick H. Schapsmeier, "Eisenhower and Agricultural Reform: Ike's Farm Policy Legacy Appraised," *American Journal of Economics and Sociology* 51:2 (April 1992), 147–59; Richard M. Flanagan, "The Housing Act of 1954: The Sea Change in National Urban Policy," *Urban Affairs Review* 33:2 (November 1997), 265–86; Eric M. Patashnik, *Putting Trust in the US Budget: Federal Trust Funds and the Politics of Commitment* (New York: Cambridge University Press, 2000), ch. 6.

18. On the murderers: Ginger Strand, *Killer on the Road: Violence and the American Interstate* (Austin: University of Texas Press, 2012). On the zebra mussels: Ronald Stagg, *The Golden Dream: A History of the St. Lawrence Seaway* (Toronto: Dundurn Press, 2010), pp. 238–39.

19. Daniel P. Moynihan, "Policy vs. Program in the '70's," *The Public Interest* (no. 20, Summer 1970), 90–100, quotations at 94.

20. See David Alan Aschauer, "Is Public Expenditure Productive?" *Journal of Monetary Economics* 23:2 (March 1989), 177–200; Edward M. Gramlich, "Infrastructure Investment: A Review Essay," *Journal of Economic Literature* 32:3 (September 1994), 1176–96; Catherine J. Morrison and Amy Ellen Schwartz, "State Infrastructure and Productive Performance," *American Economic Review* 86:5 (December 1996), 1095–1111; John G. Fernald, "Roads to Prosperity? Assessing the Link between Public Capital and Productivity," *American Economic Review* 89:3 (June 1999), 619–38.

21. Robert J. Shiller, "Inspiring Economic Growth," *Project Syndicate,* available at www.project-syndicate.org/commentary/economic-growth-after-2008-global-financial-crisis-by-robert-j—shiller-2015-05 (May 18, 2015).

22. Greg Ip, "Quality of Infrastructure Spending Needs Focus," *Wall Street Journal,* May 21, 2015, p. A2.

23. C. Vann Woodward, *Thinking Back: The Perils of Writing History* (Baton Rouge: Louisiana State University Press, 1986), p. 87. Quotation made available in Michael Barone, *Our Country: The Shaping of America from Roosevelt to Reagan* (New York: Free Press, 1990), p. 211.

24. On the war's impact in the United States: Philip A. Klinkner and Rogers M. Smith, *The Unsteady March: The Rise and Decline of Racial Equality in America* (Chicago: University of Chicago Press, 1999), ch. 6.

25. See, for example, Joshua Bloom, "The Dynamics of Opportunity and Insurgent Practice: How Black Anti-colonialists Compelled Truman to Advocate Civil Rights," *American Sociological Review* 80:2 (2015), 391–415.

26. Robert J. Fleegler, "Theodore G. Bilbo and the Decline of Public Racism, 1938–1947," *Journal of Mississippi History* 68:1 (2006), 1–28.

27. See Terrence M. Cole, "Jim Crow in Alaska: The Passage of the Alaska Equal Rights Act of 1945," *Western Historical Quarterly* 23:4 (November 1992), 429–49.

28. Michael Lind, *What Lincoln Believed: The Values and Convictions of America's Greatest President* (New York: Random House, 2004), pp. 231–32.

29. On Canada: "Canada's First Nations Peoples Given Voting Rights: March 31, 1960," available at www.danielnpaul.com/CanadianVotingRights-1960.html. On Australia: Stephen Castles, Bill Cope, Mary Kalantzis, and Michael Morrissey, *Mistaken Identity: Multiculturalism and the Demise of Nationalism in Australia* (Sydney: Pluto Press, 1988), p. 21.

30. On the United States, see for example Robert Mann, *The Walls of Jericho* (New York: Harcourt Brace, 1996), ch. 18. On Canada: Richard J. F. Day, *Multiculturalism and the History of Canadian Diversity* (Toronto: University of Toronto Press, 2000), pp. 186–87. On Australia: John Chesterman, *Civil Rights: How Indigenous Australians Won Formal Equality* (St. Lucia: University of Queensland Press, 2005), ch. 2.

31. Gwenda Tavan, *The Long, Slow Death of White Australia* (Melbourne: Scribe, 2005), p. 115.

32. On Australia: Castles et al., *Mistaken Identity,* pp. 51–55; On Canada: Day, *Multiculturalism,* pp. 185–86. On New Zealand: Jock Phillips, "History of Immigration," *Te Ara—the Encyclopedia of New Zealand,* updated August 21, 2013, available at www.TeAra.govt.nz/en/history-of-immigration/page-15.

33. James Walsh, "Navigating Globalization: Immigration Policy in Canada and Australia, 1945–2007," *Sociological Forum* 23:4 (December 2008), 786–813, at 796. The similarity of immigration policy change in the 1960s in three Anglophone coun-

tries is discussed in Jill Vickers and Annette Isaac, *The Politics of Race: Canada, the United States, and Australia*, 2nd ed. (Toronto: University of Toronto Press, 2012), p. 104–06.

34. On the Labor Party's turnaround: Tavan, *Long, Slow Death*, pp. 18–19, 35, 116, 127–28, 155, 191–92, 198–202. On the left parties pressing universalistic rights in Australia, New Zealand, and the United States after World War II, see Thomas Janoski, *The Ironies of Citizenship: Naturalization and Integration in Industrialized Countries* (New York: Cambridge University Press, 2010), p. 247.

35. On Chinese exclusion, see Daniel J. Tichenor, *Dividing Lines: The Politics of Immigration Control in America* (Princeton, NJ: Princeton University Press, 2002), ch. 4. On Wilson and Versailles: Michael L. Krenn, *The Color of Empire: Race and American Foreign Relations* (Washington, DC: Potomac Books, 2006), pp. 64–65; Margaret MacMillan, *Paris 1919: Six Months that Changed the World* (New York: Random House, 2002), pp. 316–21.

36. The analogy is drawn in Adam Fairclough, "Was the Grant of Black Suffrage a Political Error? Reconsidering the Views of John W. Burgess, William A. Dunning, and Eric Foner on Congressional Reconstruction," *Journal of the Historical Society* 12:2 (June 2012), 155–88, at 173–74.

37. See, for example, Bruce Ackerman, *We the People:* vol. 3, *The Civil Rights Revolution* (Cambridge, MA: Belknap Press, 2014).

38. See Gregory J. Wawro and Eric Schickler, *Filibuster: Obstruction and Lawmaking in the U.S. Senate* (Princeton, NJ: Princeton University Press, 2006), pp. 76–87; Gregory Koger, *Filibustering: A Political History of Obstruction in the House and Senate* (Chicago: University of Chicago Press, 2010), pp. 74, 118–19, 123, 154–57.

39. See David R. Mayhew, *Partisan Balance: Why Political Parties Don't Kill the U.S. Constitutional System* (Princeton, NJ: Princeton University Press, 2011), pp. 98–99.

40. Koger, *Filibustering*, p. 154.

41. For one elaboration of this analysis, see Mayhew, *Partisan Balance*, pp. 98–101. On the southern resistance in the Senate, see Keith M. Finley, *Delaying the Dream: Southern Senators and the Fight against Civil Rights, 1938–1965* (Baton Rouge: Louisiana State University Press, 2008).

42. See John David Skrentny, *The Ironies of Affirmative Action: Politics, Culture, and Justice in America* (Chicago: University of Chicago Press, 1996), chs. 4–6; Sunita Parikh, *The Politics of Preference: Democratic Institutions and Affirmative Action in the United States and India* (Ann Arbor: University of Michigan Press, 1997), chs. 4, 5;

Hugh Davis Graham, *Collision Course: The Strange Convergence of Affirmative Action and Immigration Policy in America* (New York: Oxford University Press, 2002), ch. 4; Dean J. Kotlowski, "Richard Nixon and the Origins of Affirmative Action," *The Historian* 60:3 (March 1998), 523–41. Anthony S. Chen, *The Fifth Freedom: Jobs, Politics, and Civil Rights in the United States, 1941–1972* (Princeton, NJ: Princeton University Press, 2009), ch. 5. Chen assigns a leadership role to the courts, too.

43. Skrentny brings out the public order theme in *The Ironies of Affirmative Action,* ch. 4 ("Crisis Management through Affirmative Action").

44. Graham, *Collision Course,* p. 66.

45. Graham, *Collision Course,* pp. 88–92, quotation at 88. See also Parikh, *The Politics of Preference,* pp. 124–25.

46. A fascinating recent study dates with some precision the faltering in the East. The "productivity performance[s]" of Czechoslovakia and Britain are compared in time series running from 1921 to 1991. The two countries' series ran in parallel until 1980 or so, an apparent inflection point, and then the East diverged downward. Autarkic, mass-production factories were no longer a match for the developing "flexible production technology" of the West. Stephen Broadberry and Alexander Klein, "When and Why Did Eastern European Economies Begin to Fail? Lessons from a Czechoslovak/UK Productivity Comparison, 1921–1991," *Explorations in Economic History* 48 (2011), 37–52, quotations at 37, 38, chart at 45. See also Daniel Sargent, "The Cold War and the International Political Economy in the 1970s," *Cold War History* 13:3 (2013), 393–425, at 418–25.

47. On the influence of the economist's ideas: Martha Derthick and Paul J. Quirk, *The Politics of Deregulation* (Washington, DC: Brookings, 1985), ch. 2; Richard H. K. Vietor, "Contrived Competition: Airline Regulation and Deregulation, 1925–1988," *Business History Review* 64:1 (Spring 1990), 61–108, at 74–83.

48. Hugh Rockoff, "By Way of Analogy: The Expansion of the Federal Government in the 1930s," ch. 4 in Bordo et al. (eds.), *Defining Moment,* pp. 148–50, quotation at p. 148.

49. Peter A. Hall, "Social Policy-Making for the Long Term," *PS: Political Science and Politics* 48:2 (April 2015), 289–91.

50. David George, *The Rhetoric of the Right: Language Change and the Spread of the Market* (New York: Routledge, 2013), pp. 2–6.

51. Marion Fourcade-Gourinchas and Sarah L. Babb, "The Rebirth of the Liberal Creed: Paths to Neoliberalism in Four Countries," *American Journal of Sociology* 108:3 (November 2002), 533–79.

52. Francis G. Castles, "The Dynamics of Policy Change: What Happened to the English-speaking Nations in the 1980s," *European Journal of Political Research* 18 (1990), 491–513.

53. Shaun Goldfinch, "Paradigms, Economic Ideas, and Institutions in Economic Policy Change: The Case of New Zealand," *Political Science* 52:1 (June 2000), 1–21; Johan Christensen, "Bringing the Bureaucrats Back In: Neo-Liberal Tax Reform in New Zealand," *Journal of Public Policy* 32:2 (August 2012), 141–68.

54. On Reagan's role, see for example Monica Prasad, "The Popular Origins of Neoliberalism in the Reagan Tax Cut of 1981," *Journal of Policy History* 24:3 (2012), 351–83; Robert J. Samuelson, *The Great Inflation and Its Aftermath: The Past and Future of American Affluence* (New York: Random House, 2008), ch. 4.

55. Samuelson, *Great Inflation and Its Aftermath*, ch. 4.

56. Derthick and Quirk, *Politics of Deregulation*, p. 53.

57. Vietor, "Contrived Competition," p. 81.

58. Robert E. Gallamore and John R. Meyer, *American Railroads: Decline and Renaissance in the Twentieth Century* (Cambridge, MA: Harvard University Press, 2014), ch. 9, quotation at p. 235. See also Mark H. Rose, Bruce E. Seely, and Paul F. Barrett, *The Best Transportation System in the World: Railroads, Trucks, Airlines, and American Public Policy in the Twentieth Century* (Columbus: Ohio State University Press, 2006), chs. 7, 8.

59. David Vogel, *Fluctuating Fortunes: The Political Power of Business in America* (New York: Basic Books, 1989), pp. 169–72; Richard H. K. Vietor, "Government Regulation of Business," ch. 16 in Stanley L. Engerman and Robert E. Gallman (eds.), *The Cambridge Economic History of the United States*, vol. 3, *The Twentieth Century*, at pp. 995–1008.

60. Michael J. Graetz, *The End of Energy: The Unmaking of America's Environment, Security, and Independence* (Cambridge, MA: MIT Press, 2011), pp. 104–15, 147–50; Richard H. K. Vietor, *Energy Policy in American since 1945: A Study of Business-Government Relations* (New York: Cambridge University Press, 1984), pp. 258–70, 306–11; R. Douglas Arnold, *The Logic of Congressional Action* (New Haven, CT: Yale University Press, 1990), pp. 231–41, 248–59.

61. Vogel, *Fluctuating Fortunes*, pp. 174–76, quotation at p. 174. See also Judith Stein, *Pivotal Decade: How the United States Traded Factories for Finance in the Seventies* (New Haven, CT: Yale University Press, 2010), pp. 192–204.

62. M. Stephen Weatherford with Thomas B. Mayhew, "Tax Policy and Presidential Leadership: Ideas, Interests, and the Quality of Advice," *Studies in American Political Development* 9 (Fall 1995), 287–330, at 314–20.

63. Morton Kondracke and Fred Barnes, *Jack Kemp: The Bleeding Heart Conservative Who Changed America* (New York: Sentinel, 2015), chs. 2, 3.

64. See Prasad, "Popular Origins."

65. Derthick and Quirk, *The Politics of Deregulation,* chs. 3–5, 7; Vietor, "Contrived Competition," 74–83; Rose et al., *Best Transportation System in the World,* chs. 7–8; Gallamore and Meyer, *American Railroads,* ch. 9; Andrew Downer Crain, "Ford, Carter, and Deregulation in the 1970s," *Journal of Telecommunications and High Technology Law* 5 (2006–07), 413–36.

66. Vietor, "Contrived Competition," 82; Derthick and Quirk, *Politics of Deregulation,* p. 147.

Chapter 6. The Climate and the Debt

1. David Vogel, "The Hare and the Tortoise Revisited: The New Politics of Consumer and Environmental Regulation in Europe," *British Journal of Political Science* 33:4 (2003), 557–80, quotation at 557.

2. David R. Mayhew, *Partisan Balance: Why Political Parties Don't Kill the U.S. Constitutional System* (Princeton, NJ: Princeton University Press, 2011), ch. 2 and appendix.

3. In general, see David Vogel, "The 'New' Social Regulation in Historical and Comparative Perspective," in Thomas K. McCraw (ed.), *Regulation in Perspective: Historical Essays* (Cambridge, MA: Harvard University Press, 1981); Richard A. Harris, "A Decade of Reform," ch. 1 in Harris and Sidney M. Milkis (eds.), *Remaking American Politics* (Boulder, CO: Westview Press, 1989); Prasad, *Land of Too Much,* p. 19; David R. Mayhew, *Divided We Govern: Party Control, Lawmaking, and Investigations, 1946–2002* (New Haven, CT: Yale University Press, 2005), pp. 85–87 and Table 4.1; Richard H. K. Vietor, "Government Regulation of Business," ch. 16 in Stanley L. Engerman and Robert E. Gallman (eds.), *The Cambridge Economic History of the United States,* vol. 3, *The Twentieth Century,* pp. 988–95.

4. For the "regulatory laggard" phrase, see Vogel, "Hare and the Tortoise Revisited," p. 578.

5. James K. Hammitt, Jonathan B. Wiener, Brendon Swedlow, Denise Kall, and Zheng Zhou, "Precautionary Regulation in Europe and the United States: A Quantitative Comparison," *Risk Analysis* 25:5 (October 2005), 1215–28, with reference at 1224–26, quotation at 1224.

6. Jon Hovi, Detlef F. Sprinz, and Guri Bang, "Why the United States Did Not Become a Party to the Kyoto Protocol: German, Norwegian, and US Perspectives,"

European Journal of International Relations 18:1 (March 2012, first published December 7, 2010), 129–50.

7. Insightful discussions appear in David Vogel, "The Transatlantic Shift in Health, Safety, and Environmental Risk Regulation, 1960 to 2010," paper presented at the annual conference of the American Political Science Association, 2011; David Vogel, *The Politics of Precaution: Regulating Health, Safety, and Environmental Risks in Europe and the United States* (Princeton, NJ: Princeton University Press, 2012), pp. 34–42, 134–42, 151–52.

8. See for example Justin Gillis, "What to Make of a Warming Plateau," *New York Times,* June 11, 2013; Hayley Dixon, "Global Warming? No, Actually We're Cooling, Claim Scientists," *The Telegraph,* September 8, 2013, available at www.telegraph. co.uk/news/earth/environment/climatechange/10294082/Global-warming-No-actually-were-cooling-claim-scientists.html.

9. See Cass R. Sunstein, "People Don't Fear Climate Change Enough," available at www.bloombergview.com/articles/2013-08-27/people-don-t-fear-climate-change-enough. For a rounded discussion of the various difficulties, see Thomas Bernauer, "Climate Change Politics," *Annual Review of Politics* 16 (2013), 421–48, at 423–26.

10. Berit Kvaløy, Henning Finseraas, and Ola Listhaug, "The Publics' Concern for Global Warming: A Cross-National Study of 47 Countries," *Journal of Peace Research* 49:1 (2012), 11–22, at 16. See also Vogel, "Transatlantic Shift," pp. 27–28; William Nordhaus, *The Climate Casino: Risk, Uncertainty, and Economics for a Warming World* (New Haven, CT: Yale University Press, 2013), ch. 25; Rebecca Riffkin, "Climate Change Not a Top Worry in U.S.," available at www.gallup.com/poll/167843/climate-change-not-top-worry-aspx (March 12, 2014).

11. Margaret Sullivan, "After Changes, How Green Is the Times?" *New York Times,* November 24, 2013, p. SR12.

12. Vogel, "Transatlantic Shift," pp. 23–28.

13. John Gerring, *Party Ideologies in America, 1828–1996* (New York: Cambridge University Press, 1998), pp. 111–16, 152–55.

14. On Europe's ambitious standards: Vogel, *Politics of Precaution,* pp. 134–42, 147–52. On the difficulties: Stephen Castle, "European Union Proposes Easing of Climate Rules: Binding Goals May End," *New York Times,* January 23, 2014, pp. A1, A13; Vanessa Mock, "Climate Goals to Fall Short of Europe Ambitions," *Wall Street Journal,* January 18–19, 2014, p. A7.

15. Enrico Botta and Tomasz Koźluk, "Measuring Environmental Policy Stringency in OECD Countries: A Composite Index Approach," *OECD Economic Department*

Working Papers, No. 1177 (OECD Publishing: Paris, 2014), chart of index values as of 2012 at p. 26.

16. See, for example, "Sovereign Doubts: Stimulus v. Austerity," *The Economist,* September 28, 2013, pp. 72–73. See also Lawrence Summers, "America's Problem Is Not Political Gridlock," *Financial Times,* April 14, 2013.

17. Steven L. Taylor, Matthew S. Shugart, Arend Lijphart, and Bernard Grofman, *A Different Democracy: American Government in a Thirty-One-Country Perspective* (New Haven, CT: Yale University Press, 2014), pp. 326–27. The eighth G8 country is Russia.

18. See, for example, Niall Ferguson, "The Shutdown Is a Sideshow: Debt Is the Threat," *Wall Street Journal,* October 5–6, 2013, p. A11; Mary Williams Walsh, "Slow-Motion Pension Crisis Awaits 20 Nations, a Study Finds," *New York Times,* March 18, 2016, pp. B1, B5.

19. José Antonio Cheibub, "Presidentialism, Electoral Identifiability, and Budget Balances in Democratic Systems," *American Political Science Review* 100:3 (August 2006), 353–68, quotation at 353. See also Nouriel Roubini and Jeffrey D. Sachs, "Political and Economic Determinants of Budget Deficits in the Industrial Democracies," *European Economic Review* 33 (May 1989), 903–38, at 922–26.

20. On Reagan through George W. Bush: Iwan Morgan, *The Age of Deficits: Presidents and Unbalanced Budgets from Jimmy Carter to George W. Bush* (Lawrence: University Press of Kansas, 2009), chs. 4–7. One good data-rich study covering 1949 through 1995 comes up dry plotting (among other things) divided versus unified party control of the government, in its conventional binary sense, against a plausible dependent variable for fiscal balance—annual percentage change in total federal real gross public debt as percentage of GDP. There is no such relation. In the study, one wrinkle of divided party control *does* tick the statistical result in a raise-the-debt direction—whether House and Senate were of opposite parties. That situation obtained during, and only during, the three Reagan-era Congresses of 1981–86. But that finding runs short on intuitive real-world logic, in a sense it stems from only one reading, and my guess is that it wouldn't keep performing absent inspired corner-shaving in any investigation updated to include the pair of instances of House-versus-Senate party splits that have occurred more recently: during the bulk of the first two-year interval of George W. Bush's first term in 2001–02, and during Obama's second and third Congresses of 2011–2014. See George A. Krause, "Partisan and Ideological Sources of Fiscal Deficits in the United States," *American Journal of Political Science* 44:3 (July 2000), 541–59. The 1981–86 finding is not a leading motif in this impressive article.

21. Klaus Armingeon, "The Politics of Fiscal Responses to the Crisis of 2008–2009," *Governance* 25:4 (October 2012), 543–65, at 549.

22. Damian Raess and Jonas Pontusson, "The Politics of Fiscal Policy during Economic Downturns, 1981–2010," *European Journal of Political Research* 54 (2015), 1–22, at 7.

23. On the arithmetic of the Budget Control Act: Naftali Bendavid and Carol E. Lee, "Leaders Agree on Debt Deal," *Wall Street Journal,* August 1, 2011, p. A1; CQ Staff, "Highlights of Budget Control Act," *Congressional Quarterly Weekly,* August 8, 2011, pp. 1761–62. On the "fiscal cliff" measure yielding the $600 billion bite: Jonathan Weisman, "Tentative Accord Reached to Raise Taxes on Wealthy," *New York Times,* January 1, 2013, pp. A1, A12; Zachary A. Goldfarb, "Tuesday's Tax Increase Is the Biggest in Decades," available at www.washingtonpost.com/blogs/wonkblog/wp/2012/12/31/tuesdays-tax-increase-is-the-biggest-in-decades/.

24. "A Happy New Year," *The Economist,* January 3, 2015, p. 21. These figures include all federal revenue and outlays. See also Nick Timiraos, "Deficit Falls to Lowest Level since 2007," *Wall Street Journal,* January 14, 2016, p. A2.

25. Nick Timiraos, "Despite Shrunken Deficit, Worries Persist," *Wall Street Journal,* October 19, 2015, p. A7.

26. Summers, "America's Problem Is Not Political Gridlock."

27. On the theory side: Kenneth A. Shepsle and Barry R. Weingast, "Legislative Politics and Budget Outcomes," in Gregory B. Mills and John L. Palmer (eds.), *Federal Budget Policy in the 1980s* (Washington, DC: Urban Institute Press, 1984), pp. 343–68.

28. See Louis Fisher, "Presidential Budgetary Duties," *Presidential Studies Quarterly* 42:4 (December 2012), 754–90, at 768–70; James A. Thurber, "The Dynamics and Dysfunction of the Congressional Budget Process: From Inception to Deadlock," ch. 13 in Lawrence C. Dodd and Bruce I. Oppenheimer (eds.), *Congress Reconsidered,* 10th ed. (Thousand Oaks, CA: CQ Press, 2013), at pp. 334–39.

29. Paul E. Peterson, "The New Politics of Deficits," ch. 13 in John E. Chubb and Paul E. Peterson (eds.), *The New Direction in American Politics* (Washington, DC: Brookings Institution, 1985), quotation at p. 396. Helpful for thinking about this interbranch question are the magisterial Richard F. Fenno Jr., *The Power of the Purse: Appropriations Politics in Congress* (Boston: Little, Brown, 1966); D. Roderick Kiewiet and Mathew D. McCubbins, *The Logic of Delegation: Congressional Parties and the Appropriations Process* (Chicago: University of Chicago Press, 1991), ch. 8, which does great justice to the question of anticipated reactions, branch versus branch; Sung

Deuk Hahm, Mark S. Kamlet, and David C. Mowery, "Postwar Deficit Spending in the United States," *American Politics Research* 25:2 (April 1997), 139–67.

30. R. Douglas Arnold, *The Logic of Congressional Action* (New Haven, CT: Yale University Press, 1990), ch. 7, quotation at p. 191.

31. This jibes with the logic and findings of Cheibub, "Presidentialism, Electoral Identifiability, and Budget Balances."

32. Robert P. Inman and Michael A. Fitts, "Political Institutions and Fiscal Policy: Evidence from the U.S. Historical Record," *Journal of Law, Economics, and Organization* 6 (1990), 79–132, at 96–99, 104–09, 114–22, 124. The measurement, which is complicated, reaches for strong independent presidents with popular bases. Tabbed as especially strong through 1990 are Washington, Jefferson, Jackson, Polk, Lincoln, Theodore Roosevelt, Wilson, FDR, Truman, Kennedy, Lyndon Johnson, Nixon, and Reagan.

33. Morgan, *Age of Deficits*.

34. On 1994, see Gary C. Jacobson, "The 1994 House Elections in Perspective," *Political Science Quarterly* 111 (1996), 203–23.

35. David Karol, "Congress, the President, and Elite Opinion in Historical Perspective," paper presented at Congress and History Conference, Columbia University, New York, June 21–22, 2013, pp. 18–27.

36. See James L. Sundquist, *Politics and Policy: The Eisenhower, Kennedy, and Johnson Years* (Washington, DC: Brookings, 1968), pp. 29–34; Edward R. Tufte, *Political Control of the Economy* (Princeton, NJ: Princeton University Press, 1978), pp. 8, 15–18; Ann Mari May, "President Eisenhower, Economic Policy, and the 1960 Presidential Election," *Journal of Economic History* 50:2 (June 1990), 417–27.

37. Richard M. Nixon, *Six Crises* (Garden City, NY: Doubleday, 1962), pp. 309–11, quotation at 310–11.

38. Larry M. Bartels and John Zaller, "Presidential Vote Models: A Recount," *PS: Political Science and Politics* 34 (2001), 9–20, at 15.

39. Arnold, *Logic of Congressional Action*, ch. 7.

40. Fenno, *Power of the Purse*.

Chapter 7. Legitimacy, Messiness, and Reflections

1. Matthew Soberg Shugart and John M. Carey, *Presidents and Assemblies: Constitutional Design and Electoral Dynamics* (New York: Cambridge University Press, 1992), chs. 7, 8, especially pp. 154–58, 165, quotations at p. 165.

2. See J. David Hacker, "A Census-Based Count of the Civil War Dead," *Civil War History* 57:4 (December 2011), 307–48. This revisionist research has upped the

overall death toll by as much as 25 percent over the long conventional estimate of 600,000.

3. On the guerrilla warfare, see Gregory P. Downs, *After Appomattox: Military Occupation and the Ends of War* (Cambridge, MA: Harvard University Press, 2015); Nicholas Lemann, *Redemption: The Last Battle of the Civil War* (New York: Farrar Straus and Giroux, 2007); Richard Zuczek, *State of Rebellion: Reconstruction in South Carolina* (Columbia: University of South Carolina Press, 1996).

4. For elaborations of the theoretical case regarding intensity, see Kathleen Bawn and Gregory Koger, "Effort, Intensity, and Position Taking: Reconsidering Obstruction in the Pre-Cloture Senate," *Journal of Theoretical Politics* 20:1 (2008), 67–92; David R. Mayhew, "Supermajority Rule in the U.S. Senate," *PS: Political Science and Politics* 36:1 (January 2003), 31–36.

5. See C. Vann Woodward, *Reunion and Reaction: The Compromise of 1877 and the End of Reconstruction* (Garden City, NY: Doubleday, 1956); Michael F. Holt, *By One Vote: The Disputed Presidential Election of 1876* (Lawrence: University Press of Kansas, 2008).

6. See Mayhew, "Supermajority Rule," p. 34.

7. On the full Reconstruction era: Richard M. Valelly, *The Two Reconstructions: The Struggle for Black Enfranchisement* (Chicago: University of Chicago Press, 2004), chs. 2, 3.

8. See Gary Orfield, *Congressional Power: Congress and Social Change* (New York: Harcourt Brace Jovanovich, 1975), pp. 96–103, quotation at 101.

9. For the nineteenth-century comparison, see Jürgen Osterhammel, *The Transformation of the World: A Global History of the Nineteenth Century* (Princeton, NJ: Princeton University Press, 2014), p. 417.

10. On the party system: V. O. Key Jr., *Southern Politics in State and Nation* (New York: Knopf, 1949). On the labor market: Gavin Wright, *Old South, New South: Revolutions in the Southern Economy since the Civil War* (New York: Basic Books, 1986). On the trade discontinuity, controlling for other variables: Gabriel Felbermayr and Jasmin Gröschl, "Within U.S. Trade and the Long Shadow of the American Secession," *Economic Inquiry* 52:1 (January 2014), 382–404.

11. Arend Lijphart, *Democracy in Plural Societies: A Comparative Exploration* (New Haven, CT: Yale University Press, 1977), pp. 112–13.

12. On the South African accommodation after the Boer War: George M. Fredrickson, *White Supremacy: A Comparative Study in American and South African History* (New York: Oxford University Press, 1981), pp. 194–98; Shula Marks, "War

and Union, 1899–1910," ch. 4 in Robert Ross, Anne Kelk Mager, and Bill Nasson (eds.), *The Cambridge History of South Africa*, vol. 2, 1885–1994 (New York: Cambridge University Press, 2011), pp. 187–94; Bill Freund, "South Africa: The Union Years, 1910–1948: Political and Economic Foundations," ch. 5 in Ross, Mager, and Nasson (eds.), *Cambridge History of South Africa*, vol. 2, pp. 234–42. On the Habsburg Empire, see for example Geoffrey Wawro, *A Mad Catastrophe: The Outbreak of World War I and the Collapse of the Habsburg Empire* (New York: Basic Books, 2014), ch. 1.

13. Some relevant material appears in David R. Mayhew, *Divided We Govern: Party Control, Lawmaking, and Investigations, 1946–2002*, 2nd ed. (New Haven, CT: Yale University Press, 2005), pp. 119–35, 221–23.

14. See, for example, Julian E. Zelizer, *Taxing America: Wilbur D. Mills, Congress, and the State, 1945–1975* (New York: Cambridge University Press, 1998), ch. 7.

15. The date for the 2013 item is January 1, 2013. The "fiscal cliff" deal was a last-gasp act by the Congress elected in November 2010.

16. For measures of voter backlash in the 2010 midterm election directed specifically at Obamacare, see David W. Brady, Morris P. Fiorina, and Arjun S. Wilkins, "The 2010 Elections: Why Did Political Science Forecasts Go Awry?" *PS: Political Science and Politics* 44:2 (April 2011), 247–50; Gary C. Jacobson, "The Republican Resurgence in 2010," *Political Science Quarterly* 126:1 (Spring 2011), 27–52; Brendan Nyhan et al., "One Vote Out of Step: The Effects of Salient Roll Call Votes in the 2010 Election," *American Politics Research* 40:5 (2012), 844–79.

17. James MacGregor Burns, *The Deadlock of Democracy: Four-Party Politics in America* (Englewood Cliffs, NJ: Prentice-Hall, 1963), p. 2.

18. See, for example, David R. Mayhew, *Partisan Balance: Why Political Parties Don't Kill the U.S. Constitutional System* (Princeton, NJ: Princeton University Press, 2011), ch. 2, for material on most of the relevant Congresses.

19. See the discussion in Josh Chafetz, "The Phenomenology of Gridlock," *Notre Dame Law Review* 88:5 (June 2013), 2065–87.

20. See Christopher Howard, *The Hidden Welfare State: Tax Expenditures and Social Policy in the United States* (Princeton, NJ: Princeton University Press, 1997); Sven Steinmo, *Taxation and Democracy: Swedish, British, and American Approaches to Financing the Modern State* (New Haven, CT: Yale University Press, 1993).

21. Martha Derthick, *Agency under Stress: The Social Security Administration in American Government* (Washington, DC: Brookings, 1990), ch. 4, quotation at pp. 91–92.

22. Derthick, *Agency under Stress,* p. 75.

23. Joel Best and Eric Best, *The Student Loan Mess: How Good Intentions Created a Trillion-Dollar Problem* (Berkeley: University of California Press, 2014), p. 64.

24. Robert A. Dahl, *A Preface to Democratic Theory* (Chicago: University of Chicago Press, 1956), p. 128.

25. See Richard F. Fenno Jr., *Congressmen in Committees* (Boston: Little, Brown, 1973), pp. 5–9, 35–45, 64–69, 90–91, 110–14, 135–37, 139–40, 152, 170–71, 180–84, 242–55, 281–83, quotation at p. 64.

26. The accounts are sketchy, but see Robert Dawson Kennedy Jr., "The Statist Evolution of Rail Governance in the United States, 1830–1986" ch. 5 in John L. Campbell, J. Rogers Hollingsworth, and Leon N. Lindberg (eds.), *Governance of the American Economy* (New York: Cambridge University Press, 1991), pp. 164–65; Robert E. Gallamore and John R. Meyer, *American Railroads: Decline and Renaissance in the Twentieth Century* (Cambridge, MA: Harvard University Press, 2014), pp. 56–63; Mark H. Rose, Bruce E. Seely, and Paul F. Barrett, *The Best Transportation System in the World: Railroads, Trucks, Airlines, and American Public Policy in the Twentieth Century* (Columbus: Ohio State University Press, 2006), pp. 3–4; Douglas B. Craig, " 'Don't You Hear All the Railroad Men Squeak?': William G. McAdoo, the United States Railroad Administration, and the Democratic Presidential Nomination of 1924," *Journal of American Studies* 48:3 (2014), 777–95. The question could use more work.

27. Mary Williams Walsh, "Slow-Motion Pension Crisis Awaits 20 Nations, a Study Finds," *New York Times,* March 18, 2016, pp. B1, B5.

28. See Stanley L. Engerman and Kenneth L. Sokoloff, "The Evolution of Suffrage Institutions in the New World," *Journal of Economic History* 65:4 (December 2005), 891–921, at 909–10. A variant of the measure appears in Robert E. Lane, *Political Life: Why People Get Involved in Politics* (Glencoe, IL: Free Press, 1959), pp. 16–22.

29. Charles A. Kromkowski, "Electoral Participation and Democracy in Comparative-Historical and Cross-National Perspective: A New Conceptualization and Evaluation of Voting in Advanced and Developing Democracies, 1776–2002," paper presented at the Annual Meeting of the American Political Science Association, Philadelphia, Pennsylvania, August 31, 2003, time series through the 2000 election at p. 28. Updated data through the 2004 and 2008 elections came in a later personal communication. The numbers for 2012 and 2016 seem to have slumped a bit.

30. Paul Frymer, *Uneasy Alliances: Race and Party Competition in America* (Princeton, NJ: Princeton University Press, 1999), pp. 149–54, 174–78.

31. Much of this up-and-down record is discussed in John A. Dearborn, "The Limits of the Representative Presidency: Constitutional Inversion and Its Consequences,"

Yale manuscript, February 2016. On various particulars: James L. Sundquist, *The Decline and Resurgence of Congress* (Washington, DC: Brookings Press, 1981), pp. 39–45, 51–57, 63–69, 99–103, 209–13; Eric Schickler, *Disjointed Pluralism: Institutional Innovation and the Development of the U.S. Congress* (Princeton, NJ: Princeton University Press, 2001), pp. 195–200. On the Trade Reform Act of 1974: Brandon Rottinghaus and Elvin Lim, "Proclaiming Trade Policy: 'Delegated Unilateral Powers' and the Limits on Presidential Unilateral Enactment of Trade Policy," *American Politics Research* 37:6 (November 2009), 1003–23.

32. On the Legislative Reorganization Act: Schickler, *Disjointed Pluralism*, pp. 141–50. On the importance of the inspectors general, see for example Jack Goldsmith, *Power and Constraint: The Accountable Presidency after 9/11* (New York: W. W. Norton, 2012).

Index